T0248042

A

GO BEYOND SELF AWARENESS,

CHANGED

REWIRE YOUR BRAIN &

MIND

REENGINEER YOUR REALITY

DAVID BAYER

POST HILL
PRESS

A POST HILL PRESS BOOK
ISBN: 978-1-64293-986-6
ISBN (eBook): 978-1-64293-987-3

A Changed Mind:
Go Beyond Self Awareness, Rewire Your Brain & Reengineer Your Reality
© 2023 by David Bayer
All Rights Reserved

Post Hill Press
New York • Nashville
posthillpress.com

Published in the United States of America
3 4 5 6 7 8 9 10

To Spirit, my family, my children,
my wife and to the new humanity emerging within all of us.
We are going to make it. Now let's get to work.

CONTENTS

FOREWORD

Several years ago, in the mountains of Colorado Springs, I gave a speech to a group of highly successful entrepreneurs. When I was finished, I was able to stay for one more speaker before catching my flight. That speaker was David Bayer. As he was speaking, the words I heard resonated at a deep level. It wasn't the same old personal development keynote. You know, the motivational ones that say:

> Don't give up
> You got to want it more
> Believe in yourself
> Be strong
> Don't give up on your dream
> You can do it
> Keep pushing
> Don't let anyone stop you
> It's always darkest before the dawn
> There is no try, only do...OK, so that last
> one is Yoda, but you get the point.

Immediately after David's speech, I approached him and we discussed some of the things he shared that I had never heard before. He had a powerful way of combining leading-edge concepts and putting them into simple but powerful frameworks to change your mind. He brought depth and ease to a topic that is so essential. In fact, our very happiness depends on it.

It was one of those immediate connections, and the next time we spoke, I was in an airport headed to Italy for the summer. Because I wanted to have more conversations with David, discuss some of his frameworks, and get to know him better, I invited him to my Tuscan home. He accepted.

This led to a deep friendship, and we set up regular weekly calls where we shared our life experiences, discussed various challenges, and supported each other in our personal and spiritual growth. David asked me to be the best man in his wedding, our families are close, and I consider him now to be one of my dearest friends.

I have also invested time with David's community, speaking to and speaking with the people in his programs and masterminds. Because they know this work and have done this work, I can go faster and deeper with them and consistently see they get even better results with my teachings. Why? Because they operate differently. They see things differently because of the way David has helped them rewire their brains.

That is why I am so excited you have this book in your hands.

See, we've all been duped.

Lied to.

Even taken advantage of if you will.

It is the way of the world, something I call the Consumer Condition. It is a disease of the mind where people take more than they give, living in victimhood and scarcity.

To overcome this issue, we've learned to exert massive effort, hustle and grind and hard work. But in all actuality, this only makes things worse. There are so many books out there about outlasting, outperforming, outworking, and killing yourself to gain some sense of self…or others that give vanilla, airy fairy advice about knowing your values and how goals is the key to success. Those books are a dime a dozen.

That is exactly why *this* book is so important and it has the ability to cure your mind of society's disease.

Society is built upon a false belief and construct. The belief that you have to work hard, and sacrifice, and then maybe one day you can be happy and achieve success. But what is success? And who determines success? And why can't we just be happy…now?

The same society puts up fake heroes in movies to create an impossible standard or places athletes and actors on pedestals exalting them as some symbol of perfection and an ideal to strive towards.

Look, no one is perfect.

Comparison is a trap.

Especially in the make-believe world of social media where everyone acts like life is always perfect.

But not David. There's nothing perfect about him. He tells you about his porn and drug and alcohol addiction. He shares his lowest moments and biggest lessons. He draws you in with his vulnerability and authenticity and then he gives you what's really important if you want to affect real change in your life. The one thing that's missing from so much of the hype of motivation and inspiration…

He delivers a clear and effective process that you can implement to create long-lasting, long-term results.

In a world where our mistakes and the harsh judgment of ourselves block love and diminish joy, it is refreshing and brave for someone to let us see their humanity and then unveil a framework unlocked through real world experience, heart-crushing pain, and heroic breakthroughs in the face of the most challenging moments.

This is the type of book that is required in today's world. A book about real human triumph, capability and spirit, not Artificial Intelligence. A book written not just on theory, but by someone who has transcended the most common and darkest parts of our human experience, and has been able to translate that experience into a powerful way forward for us all.

So, as you read this book, realize, no textbook can or will approach these results and no AI can replace human connection. There is so much value in shared wisdom, especially of someone who has been where we are, who has made it to the other side, and who has the capacity to share with us a map to follow through in their footsteps. As the words touch your heart and free your mind, you will see a path to progress and prosperity.

Congratulations.

An investment in yourself is always the best investment.

And congratulations for caring enough about yourself to read this book and improve your life.

You're in David's world now. You are not alone and you're about to gain the key to unlocking a new future. Enjoy.

Garrett Gunderson
Entrepreneur, Comedian, Multiple *WSJ* Bestselling Author and
NYT Bestselling Author and Semi-professional Shaman

INTRODUCTION

I finished reading the very last sentence, closed the book, took a long, appreciative look at the cover, and gave it a heartfelt kiss before placing it gently on my nightstand. My hands rested softly on my belly, and a smile stretched across my face. I lay quietly on my bed, reveling in the afterglow of the beautiful wisdom and teachings that I had received having just completed reading *Autobiography of a Yogi* by Paramahansa Yogananda.

There have been a few instances in my life where a book changed, well, everything. Maybe you've had this experience. At a time in your life when you were urgently seeking answers to questions that came from a burning desire within your heart and soul. Every once in a while, life responds with a well-timed book from an author you've perhaps never heard of, writing at a point in history you may have very little connection with, sitting down to take on the laborious process of answering the question that you've been asking. In a very real sense, they sat down to write a book just for you.

My hope is that this book will be that for you. I believe there is a reason why you and I are here together—why you've invited me into this sacred space to have what will undoubtedly be an intimate and powerful conversation miraculously relevant to what you're going through in your life right now, and to the questions you've been asking.

My wish is that this book dramatically shifts the momentum of your journey forward. That it helps you to realize you're not alone and you're precisely on the right track. That by the time we are done, your perception of your life, yourself, reality, and everything within it will be forever changed for your magnificent good. That by the end of this book the words contained herein may impact you in such a way that you'd grant the cover a little kiss. To be clear not for me, but for the elegant truths that have found their way to YOU through the extraordinary synchronicities that have drawn you to them.

You are the one asking the questions, doing the work, and having the courage to say YES to something (and to becoming someone) more. By the time we're done with this book, you'll realize that this is really a conversation between you and YOU—and that you should afford yourself a peck on your own cheek for the great work you've done. God knows we would be well served to find good reason to celebrate ourselves more, and you are worth celebrating.

What I'm going to share with you in this book changed my life forever. It has changed the lives of tens of thousands of people already, many of whom had been seeking answers for years if not decades, just like myself. Beginners, too, who had just begun asking the most important existential questions we can ask. *Who am I? What is my purpose? Is there something more? How do I experience less suffering and more joy?* It's made the difference for those who have been on the journey of personal development but have hit a plateau in their evolution—who have consumed all the information and distinctions in self-help and yet still suffer a gap in the embodiment of those principles.

While this book may contain some scientific and spiritual theory, it is not theoretical. The application of the principles in this book has, without fail, proven to produce results when applied in consistent, enthusiastic devotion. I have never met anyone so far stuck, or suffering from such deep childhood trauma, or having a long history of money or health or relationship challenges, who was not able to use the concepts in this book to powerfully and rapidly overcome their personal history to become a person reborn with a new life and new possibilities.

I was the first of my own case studies. At thirty-three years old, I was struggling with drug and alcohol and porn addiction, running a failed business, moving in and out of bad relationships, and remaining single for more than a decade. I felt spiritually disconnected and had no sense of purpose or meaning in my life. If there was a hopeless case, I was it.

The good news is that hope has nothing to do with what I'm going to share with you throughout the course of this book. You don't hope you know how to drive a car once you've learned how to drive it. You don't hope you can tie your shoes once you've already been shown how. And just as there is a series of steps or instructions we can follow to learn how to ride a bike, or build a piece of furniture, or learn how to swim, so too is there a step-by-step framework or process for elevating yourself beyond your current circumstances, which you can follow to consciously create the life you want and become the person you desire to be.

Like Jennifer, who was running a $10-million-a-year manufacturing company that had been stuck and losing money for three years. She was living with overwhelming stress and daily anxiety and on the brink of shutting down her dream business. Within a few months of applying what you'll learn in this book, she sold her company for over $20 million, moved to the Caribbean, and found the love of her life.

Or Allison, who had been depressed for over a decade, suicidal, and purposeless, having no desire to live any longer. Within a short period of time following the instructions in this book she said, "I went from not wanting to be here any longer to having an urgency to live and absolute clarity on what I'm here to do, and how to do it."

Like Nathan, a forty-two-year-old stockbroker who was feeling burned out and lifeless in both his career and marriage, fearing that the best years were behind him and living in a constant state of comparing and a deep insecurity that he just wasn't good enough. Within a few months of learning what you'll learn in this book, Nathan discovered a profound sense of self-love and appreciation, reconnected with his family and himself, and launched his own coaching and consulting company that now helps other fathers experiencing midlife burnout re-create their lives using what Nathan learned from his personal journey.

I don't know what you want for your life. But I do know that whatever it is, it's possible. If the vision is calling you, you have the tools, the resources, and the capacity within you to create the change you're looking for. All you need is a plan. Not a plan to create what you want, but a plan to *change your mind*. The solution you're seeking—more money, better health, improved relationships, greater clarity, more purpose—is already inside you. As you learn how to free yourself from the patterns of thinking that are creating the stress, anxiety, and overwhelm, you will unlock the energy, ideas, and internal resources to radically transform your life.

But how do you get there? You need an operating manual to a changed mind—a simple process to free yourself from the memories, limiting beliefs, and misunderstandings that keep you stuck in a life that's so much smaller than your birthright as a human being.

The question is complex: Can you *really* change your life?

The answer is simple: absolutely.

And this book will show you how.

PART I

Becoming Aware

1

The Setup

I had always been entrepreneurial, and while growing up, a lot of the people around me thought I'd be a successful businessman. But that was before I decided to ravage my life, my finances, and my career through the highly efficient and destructive vehicles of drug, alcohol, and porn addiction. As an overachiever, one addiction didn't quite seem enough.

So in *that* sense it seems unlikely that today I'd be running one of the fastest growing transformational companies for entrepreneurs and high performers in the world; that influencers, celebrities, and business icons would ask me to speak on their stages, be interviewed on their podcasts, or coach them personally; that I'd have a community of hundreds of thousands of the most incredibly evolved and impact-driven human beings whose lives and businesses have been radically transformed through the teachings, frameworks, and philosophies that I share; or that I'd be married to the most beautiful, intelligent, spiritually oriented, supportive, and all-around badass woman on the planet with whom I'm co-creating our business, our mission, some babies, and our life.

On paper, none of these things *should* have happened, but they did. And the story of how they happened, and keep happening, is a living example of what's possible for you, and anyone else, who says *yes* to a changed mind.

Great Expectations

I walked into the Postermat, an enormous warehouse of a store down on Prince Street in the Soho neighborhood of Manhattan, with butterflies in my stomach. I had recently graduated from Columbia University with a bachelor's in comparative literature and a secondary focus in creative writing. My dream was to become a screenwriter, and I thought what better way to get exposure and experience than to work in television. So after a dozen or so applications and a few professional strings my New York City lawyer dad had to media companies in the city, I landed an internship at one of the top cable networks. But the novelty of working in the television industry quickly wore off, and the reality of what it meant to be an executive assistant rapidly sank in.

Spending hours every day on the train to be stuck all day in a cubicle organizing file folders, transposing documents into electronic form, and compiling market research got real boring real fast. In my just-post-teenage arrogance of thinking my bosses were stupid, work was stupid, and even the idea of having a job was stupid (I may have actually been on to something there), I began entertaining dreams of starting my own business and becoming my own boss.

This was in the late 1990s, when the internet was becoming a thing and e-commerce was turning out to be more than just a fad. After a long weekend contemplating what significant contribution I could make to humanity through this bold new digital medium, it finally hit me. College students all across the country were faced with a terrible dilemma: where to find cool décor for their dorm rooms. So there I was, at the entrance to the Soho mecca of inflatable furniture, glow-in-the-dark door beads, lava lamps, posters, and strobe lights, with business plan in hand, ready to pitch Alan—the psychedelic colored-glasses-wearing hippy business owner of the Postermat—on the opportunity to put all his fine wares on the interweb. A few months later Alan and I were in business together, and I had over three hundred student reps on every major college campus in the country promoting my new online store. Within a few years I had built a thriving internet business and established myself as a young, successful internet entrepreneur. Not bad for just turning twenty-one.

From the outside, it seemed a setup for a Forbes 30 Under 30 profile. At twenty-five I leveraged my success as an internet entrepreneur to land a director position driving the web strategy for a globally famous Italian motorcycle brand, generating over $70 million in sales in the first two years and becoming the first motor vehicle company ever to sell a motorcycle online. By thirty, I had raised over $4 million to launch a search engine–based lead generation company in the financial services sector. I was dating beautiful women, driving fast cars, and was the life of the party. I was on my way to fulfilling the prophecy that others had felt about me since I was president of my high school senior class and captain of my basketball team. I was smart, charismatic, hardworking, intelligent. And I was going to be one of those business mogul dot-com billionaires.

Except that inside I felt like an absolute failure.

Every day was filled with the pressure that I had to make the next thing work, that I had to be more successful than I was before, that I might lose all that I had gained. There never seemed like there was enough time. I felt like if I wanted to get things done right I needed to do them, because nobody else could live up to my standards. I was engaged in a constant inner dialogue criticizing myself that I either wasn't doing enough, wasn't good enough, wasn't as far along as I should be, or that something bad was going to happen.

My inner critic became so intense that I ramped up my drug, alcohol, and pornography abuse just to quiet the noise inside my head—a momentary distraction. What I didn't realize at the time was that this voice in my head wasn't something that started in my thirties; it had just started to pick up steam. The reality was this inner voice had been going on for as long as I remember, which was all the way back to when I was seven years old.

David Bayer

The Seeds of Insanity

I was sitting on the concrete floor of my parents' garage putting the finishing touches on an arts and crafts project given by my second-grade teacher. The assignment was to construct a model of Mission San Juan Capistrano, a historic landmark in the city I lived in. In 1776, a group of Spanish Catholic missionaries constructed a chapel, living quarters, and acres of beautiful gardens that became the birthplace of what is now Orange County, California. Wood chips, newspaper cuttings, a colorful variety of markers and paints, balls of clay, glue, and other crafting materials were scattered around my work area in the garage. Dad and I had been working on it for a few days, and I had been left alone for about twenty minutes while he went out front to replace one of the light bulbs in a standing lantern at the end of the driveway.

I felt excited about how the project was coming along. The miniature garden, which was made from clippings of my mom's actual garden beds, resembled the real thing. The paint on the main chapel was complete, including a tiny replica of the cracked bronze church bell. I was now working on the Franciscan monks' sleeping quarters, which were connected to the main chapel. The project was nearly complete.

As I looked over our artistic handiwork, I thought how nice it would be to move the sleeping quarters over near the garden so the monks could wake up each day and walk through the gardens on their way to church. Excited by this small but meaningful modification to my design, I leaned over the chapel, grabbed the little clay sleeping quarters, and placed them down on the other side of the gardens. My dad, a towering giant of a man at six foot seven, walked back up the driveway a few moments later and stood at the entrance of the garage, arms folded, looking down at the changes I'd made to the layout.

"What'd you do there?" he asked.

"Just moved some of the buildings over to here," I said, pointing at the little makeshift buildings.

"Hmm, that's interesting," my dad replied as he scanned the miniature landscape, glancing back and forth between where the buildings used to be and the spot where I had moved them.

"You know what, why don't we put them back where they were? Over here by the chapel. I think they make more sense there," he eventually said.

My dad squatted down, picked up the tiny buildings, placed them back down near the chapel, and pushed the pieces of clay together to remold them into a single solid structure.

"This is the way it was drawn in the picture. It's best to try to make it as accurate as possible," he explained matter-of-factly.

Small, almost unremarkable moments shape the trajectory of our entire lives. As I watched my dad fix my "mistake," a seemingly benign thought occurred to me. A thought that would play a pivotal role in shaping my perception of myself, my work, and my reality for the next few decades. It happened so quietly and briefly that it took me years to remember the incident that formed the lens through which I experienced most of my adolescence and young adulthood.

In that moment in my garage, I thought to myself, *I don't know how to do it right.*

My dad was a brilliant thinker, a great problem solver. You wouldn't want to get into a Rubik's Cube or crossword puzzle contest with him, nor a legal argument. He was smart, quick-witted, highly educated, and critical. For Dad, there was a right way and a wrong way to do things, and the right way was, well, almost always his way.

It was rare that someone would do or say something in my family without my father's commentary on how it could have (and should have) been done or said better and even more rare that a comment or remark would go unchallenged. This created an environment of perfectionism, and I found myself constantly striving to do things "the right way" in order to please my father and gain his approval. My dad wasn't aware that his critical mind was creating criticized children.

My mother was the perfect yin to my father's yang. Born to an angry, embittered, and abusive anti-Semitic Latvian mother who left Nazi

Germany as a teenager, my mom grew up consistently feeling and hearing that she was never good enough. As they say, opposites attract. Mom was a worrier. She worried things would go wrong. She worried what other people would think. She worried that she wasn't doing enough or wasn't good enough. It was hard to see the dynamic between my parents—my dad always criticizing my mom and my mom worrying herself and my dad to death.

These experiences we have of our parents aren't just memories; they become highly impactful programs that shape the lens through which we experience the world and become driving forces for our own personality. The *vast* majority of our belief systems, which inform the way we perceive the world and who we are as people—our personalities—come from our observations of what our caretakers said, felt, and did when we were children. And the way these programs are formed is stunningly subtle and nuanced, which is why, as adults, we are often confused as to why we do what we do. But a close analysis of our personal history makes everything stunningly clear.

For example, my father would often spend the week working long hours and staying at a hotel in Los Angeles, which was a three-hour commute from our home. But he always made it a point to make it to as many of my basketball games as possible. On one level he was an incredibly committed dad—finding the time to balance an insanely busy and high-pressure career while also showing up for his kid. But the fact that he was generally absent from the home, in tandem with the idea that I needed to be perfect, led me to believe that in order to earn my dad's love and attention I needed to perform athletically. Over time, performance and success became a metric by which I evaluated my lovability. My mother, who cared deeply about the well-being of my siblings and me, often communicated that love through her well-developed habit of worry. This helped shape my perception that I wasn't safe and that the world was dangerous.

Because these programs can develop both overtly or subtly, we often have no memory of the offending incidents that created them. This is why we can't quite understand why at thirty or forty or fifty years old we find ourselves unable to manage our lives effectively and feel like we're actually living a life that isn't ours to live. But when we can understand that we've adopted unconscious programs or beliefs such as "there's a right way and a wrong way to do things" or "you'd better get it right, otherwise you aren't good enough and won't be loved..." well, our day-to-day anxiety and overwhelm starts to make a little more sense.

So there I was, at thirty-three years old, in a midlife crisis of addiction, stress, anxiety, and depression. I was driven by a hypervigilant nervous system constantly in fight-or-flight mode, terrified that any miscalculation I made could cost me everything (most importantly the love of others). I felt as though the achievements I had accumulated amounted to nothing more than what should be minimally expected of me. All of that, coupled with my increasingly destructive drug, alcohol, and porn abuse, became woven together into a tightly knit, suffocating feeling of hopelessness. Despite the fleeting moments where everything looked quite pleasant, maybe even desirable, from the outside, on the inside I desperately wanted to find a way out of my own life.

My story isn't any better or worse or more or less traumatic than yours. I probably had it easier than many of the people I have helped who experienced physical, sexual, and overtly abusive emotional trauma. What I've learned is that while our stories have similarities, they are also each one different. And with good reason. Each of our stories is an intelligently designed setup for, as we will explore more deeply later, putting us on a path toward achieving our own unique potential.

However, despite the different details of our stories, the programs are actually the same. Your mind is a system very much like software that operates based on the programs that are written or installed on it. To some extent *we all* feel like we're not good enough, that there's not enough time, that we're not going to do it right, that money is hard to make, or that we may end up all alone. This is very good news, because it means that once we learn how to transform the program for one person, we can transform it for *every* person, regardless of what experiences created it.

When you are able to identify the programs that are creating your personal suffering and preventing you from creating more in your life, you can uninstall them. You can learn to use your mind to rewire your own brain and permanently change the way that you think, feel, act, and perceive the world. And, when you do, you can heal your past and unlock an almost inconceivable amount of new potential. This book is the guide to the inner workings of the mind, or what I call your "mental operating system," and the key with which you will unlock the destiny you deserve.

The Missing Piece

Over the last several years, I've had the great opportunity to speak in front of tens of thousands of people and share the concepts and ideas contained within this book. I try to make it a point to spend a little time with audience members both to hear their stories and to discover what resonated most with them from my talk. Occasionally I meet people who are brand new to personal growth and who have just begun their journey into self-awareness and transformation. But more often than not I meet people who have been walking their path for decades, often far longer than myself.

After my very first presentation in front of a room full of financial advisors, a wonderfully kind woman in her mid-sixties approached me and shared something with me that would become common to the feedback I would later receive from thousands of people (although I had no idea at the time).

"I've been doing this work for decades," she said. "All the way back to Est and Werner Erhard. I meditated with the Maharishi. All the Tony Robbins programs. I've done deep healing work across so many modalities. I'm a spiritual teacher myself. But there's always been something missing."

Back then, I didn't know who or what Est and Werner were. The closest thing I knew to Maharishi was Mitsubishi.

"What's been missing?" I asked.

"I'm still not happy," she replied. "Don't get me wrong—there are many times when I am, but they are the exception not the norm. It's as if the majority of my life still has an undercurrent of...I don't know what to call it." She paused thoughtfully.

"Suffering?" I asked.

"Yes, that's a great way to describe it," she replied. "But what you just shared up there. What you just said...I have to tell you. *It's the missing piece.* It's the two-millimeter distinction I've been looking for my whole life." Her gratitude was palpable. Her eyes watered. I saw something truly beautiful in her sincerity. It was hope.

"Thank you. Thank you so much for doing this work, and for sharing so much of your own journey, and for giving me the missing piece."

Is this all there really is to this thing called life? You work hard, you try to do the right things, you do your best to be a good person, but underneath it all there's this constant hum of discontent that's interrupted from time to time with joyful moments. Is this just the maximum experience that life can give you, where true ecstasy and unshakable peace and feeling like you're in the zone is the exception and not the rule?

Maybe you're tired of living in financial insecurity and you want to learn how to master your relationship with money and live a more abundant life. Maybe you've realized there's more to life than the nine-to-five that you unconsciously stumbled your way into and you want to tap into a deeper meaning of purpose in your work and your life.

Perhaps you're a working parent and you're trying to keep all the plates spinning between your successful career and your marriage and the soccer or baseball games or dance practices and you're living each day in dread that today will be the day when all the plates come crashing down and you become exposed as anything less than the super dad or super mom you think you've got to be.

It could be that you've been struggling in a relationship or to even find one and you worry that you might never meet the partner of your dreams or that you'll be living a life of loneliness. You're doing the math on how long it's been since your last meaningful relationship and how much time you have left in this life. Maybe you're starting to feel a sense of time running out, and you fear that your best days have already passed you by.

Maybe you've been experiencing a health challenge or a series of them that has been going on for years or decades and you've gone to see all the doctors and specialists and nobody can seem to figure out what's wrong with you, and as a result you've started to give up hope that you'll ever be capable of living a "normal" life.

You're a business owner and you're fed up with the hustle and grind and the ups and downs of trying to grow your business and you know that there's got to be a better way because you sense a feeling of being trapped, unsure how to get the business to work, and therefore putting the rest of your life on hold.

Or like what happened for me, the hum has become too much to bear. You're living in a fog of depression and have found yourself checking out of the pain and discomfort of your unfulfilled life through drug or sex or food or alcohol addiction that is beginning to take you into a dark place that you fear you may never be able to crawl out of.

I want you to know that I *get it*. I've been in the depths of desperation, fear, worry, depression, and shame. I've felt lost, alone, scared, worthless, and without hope. I've been in some of the lowest places—emotionally and physically—that you can possibly imagine in this life. And I've met hundreds, if not thousands, of other human beings who have too.

And here's what I know beyond all doubt to be true: you're going to be okay.

More than okay, you're going to be great. Because the symptoms you're experiencing right now, no matter how long you've been experiencing them, are signs of an impending breakthrough, not a sentence for life. Here's what I absolutely know to be true based on my own experience and the experience of thousands of others: once you get on the path, you're going to finish the journey. You're going to make it to the other side.

There may be many times where it may not feel like it, but rest assured as long as you stay committed to that desire in you for more, the resources, the resilience, and the support you need will show up to usher you through to the other side.

There's Nothing Wrong with You

There's something powerful inside you that's emerging through the mess. At the early stages it doesn't feel so powerful—it feels more like frustration, anxiety, anger, depression, indecision, worry, and overwhelm. What's more, as you become even more aware of the negative inner dialogue and emotions, things can feel even more hopeless. A kind of self-awareness purgatory where you've become acutely aware of your limiting beliefs and negative inner dialogue but haven't yet gained the ability to shift it. And that's totally normal.

These feelings are designed to motivate you, to move you, into an equal and opposite direction toward joy, abundance, connection, ease, compassion, curiosity, mindfulness, spiritual growth, and successful achievement. In other words, where you are and how you are feeling right now *is* the way to achieving what you want. And what you want is one thing and one thing only: *more.*

That pain inside you is simply a longing for more. More health. More connection. More money. More impact. More creativity. More spiritual connection. More self-love. More self-esteem and self-confidence. More capacity to care for and support others. More living in alignment with who you are and what you're meant to truly do in this lifetime and on this planet here and now. More power to create and effect change around you rather than feeling like you're a response to your circumstances. It's a call to elevate who you've been, to transform the way you've been thinking, and to rise up into a new level of consciousness and capability so that you can have what I call a "powerful living experience." So that you can live your life in the full expression of who you are and consciously create a masterpiece life.

Your DESIRE is waking you up to the emergence of a new you. With that desire comes all the tools, resources, and capacity to achieve more than you can possibly imagine. If you are here, reading these pages, it is by no coincidence. Know that the realization of your desires is an absolute inevitability. Hold tight, my friend.

My expectation is that by the time you're done reading this book, among the many takeaways you may have, there will be one that unites you, and me, and anyone who has been through this work.

That this book will be "the missing piece."

The concepts and distinctions and stories that you read will bring together a new awareness for you of how this whole personal growth thing works and take you beyond self-help and into the attainment of your highest personal evolution. Not just conceptually, but in your real-world experience.

Not in idea. But in application.

By the time you're done, you'll be able to see how science, spirituality, and self-help come together into both the unfolding story of humanity and the unfolding story of YOU. You will experience a deeper relationship with yourself, with others, and with a power greater than yourself.

You will have crystal-clear answers to the up until now difficult-to-answer questions. You'll have a step-by-step road map to close the gap between the smallness you've been pretending to be and the immeasurable magnitude of the powerful creator you are destined to become. You'll also have the tools to not just expand your self-awareness but to actually change the way you think, rewire your habits of emotion, and create a fundamental spiritual and biological shift in who you are.

With a changed mind you will transform your relationship with everything around you. You will have absolute clarity around your purpose and why you are here. Every challenge will immediately be met with even better solutions. You will operate in a consistent state of flow knowing what to do and say naturally and easily. As you continue to eliminate the patterns of limiting beliefs that are unconsciously active in the neural networks of your brain, you will unbind that energy into a focused level of concentration that will allow you to be more present, compassionate, and powerful in every single aspect of your life. You will experience the science of transformation and what it means to awaken as ruler of your new kingdom right here, right now on earth.

This book isn't about motivation or inspiration. Although by the time you're done (and perhaps throughout) you may feel motivated and inspired.

This book isn't a regurgitation of personal development clichés and worn-out sayings. It won't tell you that you need to change your thinking or eliminate your limiting beliefs or get on with the hustle and grind. But it will teach you the scientific and spiritual principles of brain change and consciousness evolution in the simplest and most practical ways so that you can master them.

I'll remind you again: you are reading these pages by no coincidence. Now is *your* time. Your life and all the moments that comprise it have led you to the doorway of your next level, and all you need to do is step all the way through. This book and all that I share with you are the thoughts and ideas that have been transmitted onto these pages as a response to the burning beat of YOUR continued asking.

You will realize with unprecedented clarity that every moment, every challenge, every trauma, and every experience of your life has sculpted you into a perfectly designed spiritual warrior who is supremely prepared for the glory ahead. As you apply the teachings in this book to heal your mind, to transform your life, and to achieve the health, wealth, and success that is your inevitability, you also set the stage for the greatest show on earth…

Because now is *our* time. We are coming together, you and I and millions of awakened masters of change—first of ourselves and then of our world—during a period unlike any in history. We are at a crossroads at which we must make a very important decision. Will we continue down the path we are headed toward self-extinction, or will we make the evolutionary leap to the next chapter of humanity? Of you and I. And our entire species.

That answer is up to each and every one of us individually and, together, collectively. The doorway through to this next level of our evolution begins and ends with *A Changed Mind*.

2

When Life Becomes Unmanageable

I swore I'd never smoke marijuana again. It was a Sunday afternoon, and I had nothing to do. No hobbies to keep me interested, no friends to get me out of the house. I was thirty-three years old, sitting alone on my back porch, staring out across the green golf course that I lived on—worrying in quiet anguish that there was something deeply wrong with me. And that's when I picked up the phone...

It had been several weeks since I'd last smoked marijuana. I rationalized that this was a pretty solid accomplishment and just a little bit of pot on a Sunday afternoon couldn't hurt. A sort of reward for my abstinence in the prior weeks. I dialed my dealer and thirty minutes later there was a knock at the door and $100 after that I had procured myself a nice little bag of Florida's finest green. I could feel my mood shifting up a beat. I headed to the kitchen, opened up a drawer, grabbed a packet of rolling papers, and three minutes later was sitting on my back porch puffing off a tightly rolled joint. My body totally and completely relaxed. My mind stilled.

I could hear the soothing chirping of the birds in the tall fir trees that lined the golf course and the sounds of the soft breeze rustling down the green. A few thoughts popped into my head related to some work projects. For a moment I was free from the critical inner voice that usually dominated my mind. It felt good. My thoughts drifted. I found myself thinking about new business ideas. A few minutes later I found myself fantasizing about several of the women I was courting, wondering if perhaps one of them might want to come over for a few puffs and a Sunday afternoon sexual escapade. A few texts and no responses later, I cracked open my computer. After all, when the real world isn't available there are millions of escapes available with the click of a button.

I had been almost thirty days clean from looking at internet porn. Prior to that, I had been on a cycle of using it daily, sometimes multiple times in a day. My monthlong abstinence seemed like it warranted a little celebration, and what better way to reward myself than a little indulgence. Just one time. Couldn't hurt, right?

Nearly two hours later, I shut down my computer. I looked at the smoldering remains of a third joint that I had smoked. I stared at myself in the mirror on the far side of my tiny dining room and began to cry.

I was here—again. Breaking another promise to myself and doing the things I swore I'd never do again because I knew they weren't who I was and were tremendously destructive behaviors. But I couldn't stop. I felt out of control. A week here, a couple of weeks or even a month there. But eventually I'd come back to the same behaviors to sooth the inner discomfort and suffering that I didn't understand. I wasn't a bad person. I was confused. And I didn't want to live this way anymore.

In a moment of clarity I grabbed the bag of pot and headed toward the kitchen sink. I may have made one mistake, but I sure as hell wasn't going to make a second one. I unzipped the plastic bag, opened up the faucet, and filled the bag with water, making the marijuana all but unusable. After closing the bag, I grabbed my car keys off the key ring, bolted out the front door, and jumped in my car. As I sped down the road toward the entrance to my neighborhood, I knew that this time things would be different.

I'm never going to do this again. No more pot. No more porn. No more acting out. This isn't who I am, and it isn't who I'm going to be.

I came to an intersection with a grocery store and pulled around back. There near the rear wall was one of those big blue dumpsters. I jumped out of my car, flung open the giant lid, and hurled the wet bag of pot into the bin. I got back in the car, drove home, and sat quietly in my living room, relieved that I had removed the temptation from my house. A calm came over me. A renewed belief that my life didn't have to be this way. That I didn't have to be this way. And then the thoughts began.

How many times have you done this before? You're so stupid. What a failure. If anyone knew the truth about you, they'd never love you. You don't have any real friends. You're going to be alone for the rest of your life. What are you going to do now?

The shame engulfed me. I could feel my heart pound, my temperature rise, my muscles tense, and my breath quicken. The self-loathing was intolerable. I couldn't stand the inner dialogue. I couldn't stand who I was. I needed to find a way out of the noise, the pain. I glanced desperately at my computer resting on my living room table. I looked over to my car keys hanging on the key ring. The thoughts wouldn't stop.

You're never going to be the success that everyone said you should be. You're a failure.

I leapt up from my sofa without thinking. I grabbed my car keys, jumped in the car, and within minutes was standing in front of the blue dumpster behind the grocery store. I pulled myself up just high enough to fling one of my legs over the top and went tumbling into the garbage. The smell was nauseating. I crawled desperately through the rubbish, tossing open cartons of food and rotten produce left and right until there, under an open box of moldy God knows what, I found my prized possession, my water-filled bag of marijuana. I climbed out of the bin and got back into my car without a concern for the leftover food remnants that clung to my clothes and sped back home. I jumped out of the car and headed to the kitchen sink. I poured out the water, laid the marijuana out on a paper plate, and placed it in the microwave.

Minutes later, I was back in my bedroom, joint in one hand, computer in the other, immersed in a fantasy world of pornography. My mind calmed as I deepened my dysfunction and my dependency on external distractions to keep me safe from my inner dialogue and deep personal suffering.

I had been trying to manage my addiction for decades. But despite my best and strongest intentions, my behaviors were becoming more extreme and even more dangerous. In that moment, I felt more alone than I had ever felt in my entire life. I was a good guy. I wanted to do the right thing. I wanted to be successful. I worked hard, and despite that nothing really seemed to be working. I buried my face in my hands and began to cry in the desperation of seeing that my life had become unmanageable and not knowing what to do to fix it. In that moment of deep shame I asked myself a question that would become the beginning of a radical unfolding of a new life and a new me...

Is This It?

Is this all there is? You try to do the right thing. You try to be a good person. You take risks to start your own business. You work hard, but all you're left with is this deep longing for something more. To be someone more. This cancerous ache of feeling like you're not good enough or you're not doing enough, constantly comparing yourself to other people, worrying about what others think, or whether you're making the right decisions and choices in life.

I thought for a moment about most of the other people that I knew—my friends, family, my employees, colleagues. Maybe they weren't struggling with drugs or alcohol or porn like I was, but for the most part everyone seemed to be living two lives. One was a superficial social-media life of having stuff and pretending to be happy. The other was a quiet but ever-present undertone of stress, anxiety, overwhelm, and low self-esteem. An addiction to misery and insecurity. It seemed that no matter who someone was or what they had accomplished, at the end of the day, the root of just about everyone's emotional experience of life consisted of a dull ache of suffering.

Is this it?

Hitting the Beautiful Bottom

"You're an addict."

It was one of those classic psychiatrist scenes. Me on the sofa, my therapist in the chair. Dan—a straight-shooting licensed mental health counselor and addiction specialist—was staring me down.

"Yeah, I'm not sure I'd go that far," I said. "But I'm clear that I have an issue."

Dan barely let a beat skip as he proceeded to manhandle my defenses, explaining to me how it is.

"Let me explain to you what's happened. You've been using pornography since you were thirteen years old to cope with the stressors of your life. As a result you never developed healthy coping mechanisms. You love marijuana because it relaxes you. But what you're really doing is using it to check out of life and to give yourself permission to act out sexually. You've got quite a combination going on."

None of what Dan was saying to me made sense at the time, and yet it felt true.

"How many times have you tried to quit?" Dan asked.

What exactly does he mean by "quit"?

"Look, it's simple. How many times have you thought to yourself, 'I should probably stop'?" Dan pointedly asked.

I sat for a moment.

"Thousands," I finally replied.

Dan kept staring me down with his piercingly direct but trustworthy eyes.

"You're an addict, Dave. And the chemical response to sexual excitation, especially with pornography addiction, is second only to heroin. I'm not going to lie to you: this is going to be a long, difficult road."

If you've never been told you're an addict by someone who actually knows whether or not you are, it might be difficult to relate to the moment you realize that in fact you are one.

One minute you're a guy that drinks or drugs or sexes a little bit too much. The next minute someone's telling you that you've got a life-threatening disease.

Dan continued to lay out the game plan.

"No porn. No cigarettes. No alcohol. No marijuana. No masturbation. For ninety days."

"No way," I told Dan. "It's not humanly possible."

"I'm not done. You're going to go to three twelve-step meetings a week. You're going to get a sponsor. You're going to work the steps with your sponsor. You're going to stop hanging out with anyone who was part of your party scene. And you're going to meet with my lead therapist once a week and show up here every Thursday for the weekly men's group."

I was in shock. I knew that Dan was right. I had tried so many times to stop before, and my addictive behaviors were getting more and more extreme. But this wasn't going to be possible.

How was I going to run my business, travel thirty minutes to attend a meeting or therapy session almost every day of the week, and have any life outside of recovery?

"You're not going to have a life outside of recovery," Dan said plainly. "It's going to take at least eighteen months to rewire your brain."

3

It Starts with Self-Awareness

I spent the next three years working a recovery program in Sex Addicts Anonymous (SAA). If there was a single contributing factor to the development of my self-awareness, it was the work that I did to get clean and sober from porn addiction. Sex addiction is rampant in today's society. Forty million Americans regularly visit porn sites, and 35 percent of all internet downloads are related to pornography. Ten percent of US adults admit to having an addiction to internet pornography—and those are just the stats on people who admit they have a problem. Porn is mainstream and yet so taboo. The image of the sex addict is some creepy unwashed dude lurking in a basement somewhere. Nothing could be further from the truth.

I spent a good portion of those three years in rooms with thirty or forty other sex addicts at weekly Sex Addicts Anonymous meetings. We'd spend an hour listening to each other share about what happened during the course of our day or week, opening up about the challenging experiences that we had been going through in our careers or our businesses, relationships and lives, and getting connected to our emotions so that we could properly process them rather than stuff them down through our addiction. The rooms were filled with lawyers, doctors, successful professionals, stay-at-home moms, college students, religious leaders, politicians, and just about every kind of person in every kind of profession you can imagine.

For my first eighteen months, nearly every single week I'd pick up what's called a white chip. Picking up a white chip meant that I had violated my "bottom line," which consisted of looking at pornography or masturbating, which my therapist wanted me to refrain from for at least ninety days to reset my system. Other group members would pick up their annual sobriety chips, meaning they had gone one year, two years, five years, or more *without* violating their bottom lines. It was hard not to compare my beginning to their middle. It was easy to think that I was never going to be able to get any amount of sobriety under my belt. But my therapist reminded me that changing the neural networks of my brain and rewiring the pathways that I had built through sex addiction would take time.

What struck me most about the people in the rooms was both their self-awareness and their capacity to not only observe their thinking and emotions but their ability to not act upon those thoughts and feelings. In a sense it was like being in a room full of monks or Jedi masters. Over time I realized how they developed this extraordinary mental capacity—which was a far greater awareness than anyone I knew or met outside the rooms, and I experienced it firsthand. Each time I would violate my bottom line, my sponsor would ask me what it was that I was feeling or thinking just before I acted out. We'd come up with a plan for the next time that happened, and my singular focus was to execute on that plan. The plan generally consisted of calling someone else in the program, sharing with them what I was thinking and feeling, and allowing myself to be heard.

Most of the time when I followed these simple instructions, the feelings subsided along with the urge to use porn. But each week my mind would find a new way to present the stress or overwhelm or feelings of not being good enough and catch me off guard. I'd act out, pick up another white chip, then rework the process with my sponsor. Over time I learned every psychological pattern and began to see it earlier and earlier in its mental conception. This capacity to see my thoughts early on in their gestation period wasn't just limited to the thoughts that triggered my addiction but *all* thoughts. Three meetings a week, multiple phone calls a day, men's group, weekly therapy, and working the twelve steps with my sponsor, and things were starting to change for me.

Maybe you've had a similar experience. Maybe, like me, you've struggled with addictions of your own. You might be addicted to substances or food. Or maybe the addiction isn't physical but emotional or psychological. Perhaps you've been addicted to anger, making other people happy, control, feeling not good enough, or some other life-impairing habit. We all have patterns of behavior that don't serve us. What are some of yours? There's no shame or guilt in the answer. But there is a power to discover in the answer—the power to change.

A Way Out

I was eighteen months into working the program when something clicked. I was starting to tap into my intuition more deeply. Not only was I getting sober, but there were little mental hunches, ideas that would make their way into the new spaces in my mind that were now available for new thoughts. When I acted upon those hunches, good things began happening. I started to notice odd but beautiful coincidences and synchronicities occurring in my life. I'd think about someone and they would call. I'd have a situation at work where I needed a particular resource and it would easily show up. I was noticing an interconnectedness between myself, my changing thoughts, and how life was showing up for me. It felt like something magical was happening that I couldn't quite put my finger on, and as a result I became even more curious about myself, about life, how it all worked, and my role in all of it.

I finally got six months of solid sobriety under my belt, and the conversations with my therapist began shifting from just trying to get through the day to going deeper into my thoughts, emotions, and my life. I realized that I wasn't in love with the work I was doing and that I wanted to make a greater contribution and impact in the world. I wasn't sure what that looked like, but I felt, for lack of a better word, *called* to do something more. And then one day another answer showed up unexpectedly.

I was flying from Miami International Airport up to Boston to pitch a group of venture investors on another round of investment in my marketing company, a search engine optimization–based lead generation company in the financial services sector. A few years prior, after hundreds of hours of studying search engines, I had decoded the little black box of how they ranked websites at the top of their search results (not realizing at the time that my ability to understand algorithms would play a major role in the work I'd be doing in personal growth).

While I was waiting for my flight to take off, I dipped into the airport bookstore and casually browsed the titles of the books on one of the shelves. I don't know if you've ever experienced this, but sometimes it feels like a book is calling out to you. It's palpable. As if it's determined to establish a relationship with you. One such book called out to me, and instinctively I reached out and grabbed it, without looking at the front cover, and turned it over to read the description on the back.

There were four statements on the back of the book.

Life is full of suffering.

The statement resonated with me powerfully. I had never heard this word used before to describe the entire category of emotions I had been experiencing and, to a great extent, what I was seeing people experience all around me.

The suffering is going to happen to you.

I felt an immense pressure lifted off my chest, as if I had just been given permission for everything I had felt, everything I had struggled with, everything I had experienced over the first three decades of my life that I had interpreted as something being "wrong" with me. This simple acknowledgment, that the suffering IS going to happen, was liberating.

There is a way out of the suffering.

I remember thinking to myself, *Shit, it's really happening.* I had been feeling like I was in the process of being guided down a path of deeper understanding. The synchronicities and coincidences had been mounting into an undeniable pattern. Just days before, I had been asking for a sign, a teaching, an understanding to help me take the change I had been experiencing in recovery and apply it to the daily stresses and overwhelms and anxieties that I was still suffering. And now this!

The way out of the suffering is the eight-fold path of virtue.

I flipped the book over and studied the cover: *Awakening the Buddha Within* by Lama Surya Das.

The back cover was stating what is known as the Four Noble Truths of Buddhism, and the book promised an understanding of the way through and out of suffering using an eight-step structure devised by Buddha. I couldn't wait to consume the framework and was appreciative of its efficiency, four fewer steps than the twelve-step program created by Bill W. I purchased the book, jumped on my flight, and between my round trip devoured it cover to cover.

What Buddha explained was quite simple. All of our personal suffering is internal, not external. The circumstances and experiences of our life are not the cause of our emotional distress. The meaning we give the experience, or our beliefs about the experience, were the sole cause of our personal suffering. This idea was groundbreaking to me, and what was even more invigorating was that Buddha pointed to a way out, a way to transcend the daily suffering of our lives so that we could live in higher states of joy, creativity, compassion, and presence on a moment-by-moment basis.

The following day I arrived at the office with an unusual gift on my desk. Back then I wasn't a reader, nor had I expressed any interest in religious or spiritual philosophy or doctrine. So when Brian Mickey, a devout Christian who was one of our social media account managers, left a little red-and-white paperback book on my desk entitled *Kingdom Principles: Preparing for Kingdom Experience and Expansion* on top of my laptop with a little card, it came quite unexpectedly. Little did I know then that my simple question——*is this it?*—would unleash a torrent of coincidences and synchronicities, leveraging all the people and resources around me in profoundly sophisticated and delightful ways, to provide me a life-changing and life-shaping answer. That night I grabbed the little book written by Myles Munroe along with Brian's card as I packed up my things and headed home.

Have you ever had one of those experiences where a series of small coincidences began to occur, and there was a moment when you realized that something highly intelligent was unfolding for your personal benefit? That night as I crawled into bed, I brought with me the little card and the book. I opened the card and there, simply written, was a little note from Brian that said, "I thought you'd find this interesting." I cracked open the book and began to comb through the pages as Munroe began methodically explaining how the teachings of the Bible were a manual for transforming your thoughts, emotions, and your life. A framework for how to transcend the suffering of your daily life and how to become, like Christ, a powerful miracle-making creator.

> "Be not conformed to this world: but be ye transformed by the renewing of your mind."
>
> —Romans 12:2 (KJV)

Hours vanished. It was three o'clock in the morning as I read the final page, closed the cover of the book, and gently placed it on my nightstand. My thoughts raced. Something had dramatically shifted inside me as a pattern was becoming clearer. The twelve steps of Alcoholics Anonymous, the eightfold path of virtue of Buddha, the teachings of Christ were all pointing to the same universal truth: every aspect of your outer experience is a manifestation or projection of your inner world. As Buddha taught, *The mind is everything. What you think you become.* There was a way through the suffering, and on the other side, as Myles wrote, a new kingdom awaited.

The following day I took an extended lunch break and headed to a local bookstore. I had never actually been inside a bookstore before. But something was waking up inside me. I felt energized and excited, like a kid the night before Christmas filled with the joyful anticipation of something wonderful under the tree the next morning. Not knowing what, but knowing whatever it is, it's coming, and it's good. I walked quickly over to the customer care desk and waited anxiously for the person in front of me to finish with the appropriately bookish-looking woman behind the counter.

"How can I help you?" she asked.

I wasn't sure what I was looking for. All I knew was that these books and their teachings had motivated an appetite for knowing more about who I was and how I could change the way I perceived the world.

"Do you have a section here for people who are wanting to improve their lives and the way that they think?" I asked.

"You mean self-help?" she responded.

That's an appropriate name, I thought to myself. "Yes," I said.

She directed me up the escalator and to the right. I quickened my pace. As I arrived at the second floor and turned, I could see just beyond the diet and weight loss section a single row with books shelved on the left and right and a small sign above that read Self Help. As I approached the section, I noticed a small red hardcover book resting on the floor midway down the aisle. I approached the book, leaned over to pick it up, and turned it over so I could read the front cover. I laughed to myself as I read the title, which seemed so appropriate for the ambitious person seeking both spiritual and material answers to their first world problems. *Think and Grow Rich* by Napoleon Hill. I had acquired another piece of the puzzle, and the edges were now starting to fill in.

Think and Grow Rich is the #1 bestselling business book of all time. Except that it's not about business at all. It's about using the mind to create powerfully in your life. Napoleon Hill studied a handful of men, known as the Titans of the Gilded Age, who shaped the reality of the twentieth and twenty-first centuries. Encouraged by Andrew Carnegie, the steel baron, Hill personally interviewed and studied the most powerful men of the industrial era: John D. Rockefeller, Henry Ford, Thomas Edison, John Pierpont Morgan, and others.

These men grew more powerful in their wealth than nations and used their wealth, influence, and power to create, restructure, and own entire industries: finance, pharmaceuticals, media, education, military, food, transportation, and eventually tech. In effect they created the structure within which the rest of humanity operates. They were the most powerful men in history outside of, arguably, Christ himself, in terms of their lasting impact and influence in the world. Carnegie told Hill that there was a "secret" that the most powerful men in history knew and used in order to accumulate their wealth, influence, and power.

In his study of these people, Hill concluded that the secret was that "thoughts were things and powerful things at that" and, when combined with a "burning desire" and a "definite chief aim," were destined to objectify or realize themselves into the material world. These teachings along with the philosophies of other teachers considered part of the New Thought Movement—including Madame Blavatsky, Neville Goddard, Raymond Charles Barker, and later Norman Vincent Peale—became the entry point and bridge for hundreds of millions of people into what is now referred to as personal development. By the early 2000s personal development exploded into a $40 billion industry consisting of countless books, courses, seminars, live events, workshops, methodologies, frameworks, and coaching programs.

Think and Grow Rich and the revelations that Napoleon Hill shares within became one of the most significant gateways guiding millions of people onto the path of personal and (eventually) spiritual growth—the same path pointed to by Bill W., Buddha, and Christ. As Gandhi said, *A man is but a product of his thoughts. What he thinks he becomes.* And so self-help, or personal development as it has come to be known today, promises a changed mind and a changed life.

But does it deliver?

4

The Broken Promise of "Self-Help"

Think and Grow Rich was my first foray into "self-help"—or personal development. My desire to understand how I could use my mind to change my thinking, liberate myself from my own personal suffering, and transform my bank account, my business, my health, my relationships, and every area of my life became the focal point of my existence. Personal growth was my new religion.

Within the next few months I read all the foundational self-help books: *Personal Power, The Power of Now, How to Win Friends and Influence People, The 7 Habits of Highly Effective People, The 21 Irrefutable Laws of Leadership, Heal Your Life, You Are a Badass, The Surrender Experiment, The Untethered Soul, Ask and It Is Given, Change Your Thoughts Change Your Life.* I found and consumed every video I could find from Tony Robbins, Wayne Dyer, Eckhart Tolle, Deepak Chopra, Marianne Williamson, Les Brown, T. D. Jakes, Joel Osteen, and just about any spiritual interview conducted by Oprah Winfrey.

The information had the potential to change my life, and I began implementing what I could. I experienced small but incremental shifts in the way I was feeling and thinking. However, fully embodying and integrating the concepts I was learning from these great teachers was still quite challenging. I understood the promise of a new mind and a new life and a new me, but every time I'd experience a small window of breakthrough, it felt like something would show up in my life—a challenge or a problem or a tragedy—and my old way of thinking and feeling would return. I was growing in my self-awareness and my ability to tune into what I was thinking and feeling, especially now that I was no longer masking my emotions with drugs and alcohol and pornography. But in many ways, the stress, anxiety, and overwhelm of daily life—the suffering—felt even more intense in that expanded awareness. The answer, I figured, was to dive even deeper into personal growth.

I attended my first transformational event when a friend referred me to a program called Landmark. I attended the three-and-a-half-day event and experienced a profound awakening and peace as a result of the teachings and frameworks that were taught. Yet a few weeks later I slipped back into my emotional habits, experiencing occasional moments of a new happiness and joy against a backdrop of generalized anxiety and discomfort. A few months later a friend of mine invited me to attend a Tony Robbins conference. Tony was literally a modern-day Superman with inexhaustible energy and superhuman size and strength as a result of a tumor on his pituitary gland that pumped excessive amounts of human growth hormone into his enormous overgrown stature. For four days, in the midst of rock concert–like energy and music, Tony kept me and ten thousand other attendees in a peak state, open to new possibilities and new ideas and the notion that, beyond this event, life would never be the same.

Except two weeks later, it pretty much was…

I was back in the same business, the same daily routines, the same problems, and the same emotional patterns as a result of coming back home with, well, the same brain. Decades of psychological and emotional habits had worn deep grooves into the neural network wiring of my brain and nervous system. Like an appendage held in a cast for too long, my mental and emotional flexibility was limited and temporary.

For the next several months, I attended half a dozen motivational, inspirational, or spiritual workshops, each time experiencing a small window of change but each time returning to the same experience of my life with a few nuanced upgrades. I was noticing that my suffering was increasing in tandem with my awareness. I began to wonder if I was doing it wrong. Was something wrong with me? Why couldn't I fulfill this "promise" of self-development and create consistent change?

I doubled down on my reading and began getting into more religious, spiritual, esoteric, and metaphysical teachings. I read the Bible cover to cover, made an attempt at the Quran, then the Bhagavad Gita. Then Rumi. I started studying the sacred tarot, astrology, and sacred geometry and watching videos on quantum theory. Each step forward brought greater understanding while at the same time enacting even greater frustration and an awareness of just how deep my suffering truly was. Along with it came a deepening fear that I was going to be a personal development failure and perhaps never truly find happiness.

Carol, my girlfriend at the time (now wife), began to see my desperate struggle. We implemented a meditation practice and created a room dedicated to spiritual practice—a home ashram—where I had framed great spiritual teachers and masters and adorned the corners of the room with spiritual emblems, incense, and sage. A few months later, I convinced Carol that we needed to go to India to study at a real ashram, and seeing my hopeless state, she grudgingly agreed. After three weeks in an ashram committed to daily breathwork, meditation, spiritual processes, and wisdom teachings—while experiencing increasing degrees of self-doubt, confusion, and borderline depression—we agreed to travel to Tibet for a ten-day extension. After all, the Beatles experienced enlightenment there, so I might hope to as well.

From Tibet we returned home for a few weeks, and my condition worsened. I felt physically and emotionally drained. I was doubting myself and my purpose. The "promise" of self-discovery had once again gone unfulfilled. Despite all the spiritual practices and journeys that were "guaranteed" to fill me up and help me find alignment, I felt nothing but empty. Our bank account was beginning to reflect the balance of my emotional state, and seeing as we could no longer afford to travel internationally, not to mention the two weeks I'd suffered a parasitic infection from Indian street food, we agreed to spend three weeks in the most spiritually transformative place in the United States. A location where the energies themselves would transform my consciousness and liberate me from my personal suffering.

Sedona.

On our fifth day in the Arizonian spiritual mecca and having spent nearly a week meditating on red rocks and seeking spiritual liberation in supposed energetic vortexes, I dipped into one of the many crystal shops that line the main highway, seeking counsel from one of the in-store psychics and energetic experts on what mineral might pull whatever energies that were tucked away in my body perpetuating my emotional and psychological discomforts. Maybe there was something that needed to get pulled from my past. Perhaps my childhood. Maybe even a past life or another dimension. I was beyond desperate.

A teenage girl was working behind the counter. She looked up from her cell phone. "Are you here to see the Aruhuacan and Kogi Indians?"

I had no idea what she was talking about. My blank stare invited further explanation.

"They've traveled for over three weeks from their home in the Amazon. It's the first time they've left the jungle. They're going to be sharing with us what's coming up with the big 2012 shift!" she exclaimed excitedly.

I paused for a moment. Had I lost my mind? What the hell was I doing in Sedona? What was I doing with my life? Nothing seemed to be working. I felt like I was worse off than when I'd started this whole journey—from that moment in the airport when I answered the calling of that damn book. I had spent over a hundred thousand dollars and thousands of hours for what? Here I was, in some loser hippie town in the middle of the desert, dragging my poor wife along on some hopeless quest to find peace within myself, and I was more miserable and insane than ever before.

"Absolutely I'm here for the Indians. Tell me where they are."

I spent the entire weekend sitting in the Sedona High School gymnasium listening to translators for the Aruhuacan and Kogi tribal leaders who were impressing upon us the importance of respecting Madre Tierra, or Mother Earth, and how it was critical to return to nature and the sacred. Plus two bonus takeaways. Stop using crystals—you people don't know how they work. And don't masturbate as much. Fortunately both of those were no longer my problem. Nice teachings, but brain changing and suffering ending they were not.

Once you go as deep as I did into personal development, there's really no stopping. In a sense, you can't let it go, because each new teaching or seminar or experience gives a quick hit of hope and emotional freedom. Like any state-altering substance or experience, there's an addictive nature and need to go back to it. On the other hand, you hold on to that one little desperate shred of a hope that *this* time will be different and the experience, the transformation, might just be permanent.

Self-Help Purgatory

By this point, I had established a love-hate relationship with spirituality and personal growth. I desperately wanted to realize the promise of personal development, and I understood intellectually that there was a possibility of psychological and emotional liberation but had grown in my resentment for the current model. I felt lured into a personal development purgatory where I was now acutely aware of my limiting beliefs but left without the proper tools, frameworks, or methods to actually change my habit of thought. I got to the point where I didn't want to read another book, I didn't want to watch another motivational video, and I didn't want to attend another *hoo-rah-rah* seminar.

And I realized that I wasn't alone.

Over the course of my wild ride into self-help, I had built some wonderful friendships with other souls on the path to "awakening." In my conversations with them I saw that they too were experiencing the same kind of struggle, the same unfulfilled promise, and the same feelings that there was something wrong not with the current model of personal growth but with themselves. We were all starting to feel broken in personal development.

Have you ever had a thought like, *I know I should have more gratitude,* but you don't. That you know you should be asking better questions and better managing your inner dialogue, but you can't. That you know you should have faith instead of fear, but you don't. What happens in these moments of awareness is that the mind takes over and you begin to judge yourself for, well, sucking at your own personal growth.

What I've learned now nearly a decade later is that THIS IS the process of the current personal development model. Personal Development 1.0 provides the foundation. It creates an intellectual understanding upon which you can then build true change and transformation. It plays a critical role in setting you up, and in its limited form it also creates a burning, oftentimes seemingly desperate desire to find a way to catalyze REAL transformation. The unrealized promise creates a powerful awareness and desire for the realization—the making real—of an actual evolution of your own consciousness. A desire to develop the capacity to actually use your mind to control and rewire your own brain. And as that desire grows, along with the mounting desperation, a bridge appears to take you to the other side.

You may have never sat for a weekend in Sedona with an ancient Amazonian tribe or dragged the woman or man you love halfway around the world desperately seeking a solution to your personal suffering. But if you're here, you can probably relate to the broken promise of personal development. Or if you're new to the conversation, you've just gotten a glimpse of what the road ahead may have looked like. The good news is that all of the great psychological, motivational, and spiritual teachings that have laid the foundation for this conversation have evolved. Now, we have an ever-increasing understanding of the mind, consciousness, neuroscience, and human behavior. We are entering into an era of Personal Development 2.0 that takes the conceptual understandings of the past and distills them into practical tools and frameworks that will allow you to embody, become, and realize your full potential. A personal technology to enable you on a moment-by-moment basis to use your mind to change your brain and rewire yourself. Welcome to Personal Development 2.0.

Where to Start

In order to realize a change in our lives and ultimately to unlock the full potential of our greatness, we have to know where to start.

For many, that's the challenge with personal growth: not knowing where to start.

If you were committed to losing weight you'd certainly know where to begin. Whether you *actually* followed the process isn't guaranteed, but the process itself is pretty straightforward. You'd take a look at your diet and see what tweaks you would need to make in order to meet your goals. You'd hire a trainer or create a workout regimen that was designed to achieve the body mass and type you intended. You would have a proven framework that you could apply, and if you executed each step of the process consistently you would in great likelihood produce the desired results.

If you wanted to write a book like this one, you'd follow a process too. First you might sit down and get clear on what topic you wanted to write about. Then you'd identify who the reader was so you could establish clarity on how to communicate the topic. Then you'd create a detailed outline and after that create a writing schedule specifically designed around your writing speed and best creative process. Perhaps then you'd establish some sort of accountability structure to ensure you actually executed on the plan and, after some period of time, unless you deviated from the plan, those actions would produce the desired result: a book.

So where do we start when what we want is to end our personal suffering and live the life we've always dreamed of? Is it possible that liberating our minds and creating an extraordinary life could have a simple one-two-three framework as well?

Our thoughts, feelings, the various challenges and daily stressors of our lives, the vision we have for something better—all these elements of our daily reality often converge and meld together into what feels like one of those time-lapse clips of a New York City square block, moving too quickly to make out anything clearly, where there is little space or time to get enough of a foothold to make any sense of it. Everything seems a blur. From the inside looking out, your life, emotions, and mind can feel like a big ball of knotted yarn with no clear thread with which to begin the untying process.

But the behavior of all humans, yourself included, is governed by a simple operating system that dictates your thoughts, emotions, actions, and ultimately the total sum of your life. Understanding how this system works is necessary for creating change in your life. You have a manual for how your TV operates, your phone, your automobile, but no one ever gave you a manual to *your* operating system. This book is that manual.

If you're reading this book, it's because you want to improve an aspect of your life. What you'll soon learn is that the change you are seeking is achieved by a change in your *inner* climate, your mental attitude, not a change produced as a direct result of activity or action in the *external* world. If that's true, which we will establish as fact, then it would make sense that we should begin to take a look at the changes you desire. That should be the starting point.

If you can, through consistent application of the principles contained within this book, create a change in just *one* area of your life, then by extension you must be able to create changes in *all* areas of your life. Having what you want is your natural right. Not having what you want, and the suffering that accompanies that experience, is an indication that there is some form of resistance that needs to be identified and removed. There is a program on your operating system that needs to be uninstalled and replaced with a program that is conducive to creating what you want. Whether that's a material, emotional, or spiritual desire—more money, more joy, or more connection—is irrelevant. What most people don't realize is that creating what you want is not about figuring out how to create it; it's about identifying the resistance and removing it. As soon as you are able to remove the program, the result you seek is 100 percent inevitable.

5

The Inner Conflict

"Nature needs no help, just no interference."
—B. J. Palmer, chiropractic pioneer

What do you want? Seems like a pretty straightforward question. But the vast majority of the time, when I ask someone what they want, they have one of two responses. They either immediately begin listing off all the things they *don't* want in their life: *I don't want to be alone. I don't want my business to fail.* Or they give me one or two things they desire before pivoting into a list of reasons why they don't have it: *I want to find love, but I don't have time to date. I want to have a great career, but I'm afraid I don't have any talent.*

The "what do you want" exercise teaches us an important lesson. In any area where we want to create change, we tend to focus on the *absence* of what we desire more than the desire itself. There's a reason for that.

Human beings are meaning-making machines. Meaning is a fundamental feature of our ability to *survive*. If we are at risk of death or harm, our sympathetic nervous system kicks in and we move into fight, flight, or freeze mode. If we are in safety, joy, or pleasure, we move into a parasympathetic response, or rest and relaxation. Which switch gets flipped depends on the meaning you're giving your experience. But because it's a matter of life or death, human beings have a natural inclination to lean toward a danger-based interpretation vs. a pleasure- or solution-based interpretation. We tend to focus on "what's wrong."

So when we set goals, or we do our vision boards, or we simply answer the question of "what do we want," within a very short period of time we begin to notice the absence of what we want and unconsciously and automatically give meaning to that absence. We tend to focus on the negative even when we're desiring the positive. If you want to make more money, the odds are that you're noticing the absence of the financial abundance. If you're experiencing a health challenge and you want to be vibrant and healthy, it would seem natural to be paying more attention to your sickness and wanting to "solve" it than paying attention to the invisible potential of your health. If you want to be in a great relationship but the relationship that you're in is lacking passion and connection and intimacy, you're more likely to pay attention to the evidence you have of your poor relationship than to direct your attention toward its improvement. We have the natural tendency to be consumed by problems rather than potential—the threat vs. the opportunity.

The One Thing

My simple question to you is, What do you want? More specifically, what do you want *most*? I'm certain you desire many things, but there is likely one thing in your life right now that will create more joy, more peace, more excitement than anything else in this moment once you have it. And the absence of it is creating more stress, more anxiety, more sadness, more anger, and more overwhelm than anything else in your life. Having it will create happiness, and not having it is creating suffering for you.

Perhaps you want to get out of your depression. Perhaps you want to have a private plane or buy yourself a yacht. Perhaps you want to have a baby or find a partner to have a baby with. Maybe you'd like to be able to spend more time in nature, or travel the world, or donate more to your favorite charity, or overcome the grief you've been experiencing from the loss of a loved one. To overcome an ongoing health challenge. To generate more leads and income for your business. To be financially free. What it is does not matter. *Identifying* what it is does. I want you to think of this thing that you desire above all else in your life right now as your "One Thing."

What's your One Thing?

What's the Problem?

My next question is, again, a simple one. The starting point is, What do you want? The next step on the path is, What's the problem?

Why can't you be, do, or have this thing? What's been preventing you from creating this in your life up until now? I don't want you to overthink it. I want you to listen to and tune in to that inner voice in your head. Every time you've thought about this thing—the bigger bank account, the larger business, the incredible relationship, the recovery from a loss, the healing of the disease—whatever your One Thing is, every time you think about this thing your brain is automatically giving a meaning to the *not* having of it.

When *you* think about your One Thing, what are all the reasons that automatically, spontaneously, and almost instantly come up for you explaining, justifying, and rationalizing why your One Thing hasn't happened yet? *That* inner voice. The one that says things like: *Money is hard to make. She's never going to change. If you want to do it right, you have to do it yourself. Nobody has ever recovered from this. It didn't work out before. I didn't have a chance to say goodbye. I don't know how to do this. It's too risky. I may not do it that well. I'm not good enough. There's not enough time.*

I know you may have *some* beliefs that this *will* happen for you or you *will* create this thing, or that you *are* in process and progress and that it *will* happen soon. But I'm also certain there is an inner resistance or doubt, an inner dialogue, that is actively explaining why it hasn't happened yet. How do I know? Because if there wasn't, you wouldn't be experiencing any suffering around it and more likely, you'd already have it.

There's a beautiful simplicity to this entry point into your transformation. If the key to creating a life you want, to having what I would call a powerful living experience—a life where anything is possible, where financial and health and relationship abundance is your birthright and comes easily, where you have the freedom to focus your time on the things you enjoy, to unlock the genius inside you and to translate that genius into some form of outward expression that you get paid for, and to live your life in joy, peace, and calm while feeling consistently connected to yourself, others, and a spiritual power inside and outside yourself—if the key to *that* is identifying and eliminating the programs and limiting beliefs you adopted when you were a child, which are stored in the recesses of your unconscious mind yet shape your daily experience, perception, and possibility...

Then the question must be, How do you become *aware* of what you're not yet aware of? How do you identify the psychological and emotional programs holding you back? How do you become more self-aware?

The answer is quite simple.

Identify what you want, and listen to the internal dialogue in your mind for the reasons and beliefs for why it hasn't happened yet. Your *explanation*—the meaning you give for the absence of what you want—is what you unconsciously believe about that area of your life.

Said another way, the reason you don't have more money in your bank account isn't because money is hard to make, it's because you *believe* money is hard to make.

The reason your health challenge isn't going away isn't because you haven't found a solution to your health problem, it's because you *believe* that it can't go away without you finding a solution or because you believe there may be no solution.

The reason you haven't met the person of your dreams isn't because there aren't any good ones left, it's because you *believe* there aren't any good ones left.

Identifying what you want and then observing your own thinking about why you don't or can't have it is the key to unlocking and accessing the unconscious beliefs and programs that are the real and only reason you haven't yet achieved or created your One Thing yet. In fact, they are the *only* reason you don't yet have *everything* you desire. And the journey to the next evolution of your personal growth begins by mapping out all your dreams, desires, and the vision you have for your life and to look at the thoughts and beliefs that are *not* in alignment with those outcomes. These original beliefs have shaped your experience and lens of perception for decades, so much so that they have in some ways become fact, or inherently true, for you. But they are not, in fact, fact. They are flexible. And as you learn how to transform the limiting beliefs that are stored in your inner reality, you will begin to radically transform the results in your outer world.

In any area of your life where you are experiencing frustration, disappointment, scarcity, anxiety, overwhelm, or any negative emotional state...

Where you desire to be, do, or have something but have been unable to achieve it...

Where there is a gap between where you are and the vision or dream you have for where you want to be...

There is only one thing preventing you from closing that gap, from creating that thing, from experiencing more joy, peace, abundance, and connection.

The problem that you think you have—that there isn't enough time, or that achieving success is hard, or that others have more resources than you—isn't really the problem.

The problem is that you have what I call an Inner Conflict.

Inside you there is a psychological and emotional incongruence. On one hand you want something. On the other hand you *believe and feel* that it's not possible to have it. On one hand you want to pursue your dream and start your own business. On the other hand you believe it's too risky. You want to find a life partner while simultaneously believing all the good ones are already taken. You want to discover your purpose, but you believe you have no idea what you want to do or that perhaps you don't even have one. In other words, the problem is not the problem. The problem is what you *think* about the problem. What you believe is in direct conflict with what you want to achieve—*this* is your Inner Conflict.

The problem is not the problem. The problem is what you think about the problem.

The human being operating system is designed to produce results in alignment with one thing and one thing only: what you think. When you desire something but unconsciously believe you can't have it—in other words, when you experience doubt, fear, or disbelief as a result of your own, limited, past experience of what is or is not possible or how things must or must not be done or accomplished—you create conflict within yourself. Your feelings are evidence of this Inner Conflict. Stress, anxiety, overwhelm, jealousy, sadness, depression, and fear—what I call "suffering"—are all symptoms that there is an Inner Conflict at play.

Your ability to create what you want or to change the momentum of your life requires a new focus and a new energy. When you desire something but believe it's not possible, you expend all that creative energy on bad feeling emotions. Rather than having creative and productive ideas arising from joyful and excited states, the focus on the Inner Conflict wraps you up, consuming your time, attention, and energy and, as a result, perpetuating your current circumstances rather than creating something new.

The good news is that once you identify your Inner Conflicts, which is accomplished by the simple process of determining what you want and then identifying why you believe it can't happen, you've now identified the only thing preventing you from achieving that which you desire: *a limiting belief.*

Once you become aware of a belief that is holding you back, you can use the tools and technologies that I'm going to teach you to transform that belief; to uninstall the memory and to reinstall a new one; to consciously architect your perception of the world so it is in alignment with the desires and dreams and goals that you have.

To use your mind to rewire your own brain.

In order to do this, two things are necessary. First, you must understand the philosophy and science of how and why you operate the way you do. Why is this important? Because it will provide you with the unshakable certainty that in fact, as Buddha said, the *mind* is *everything*, what you *think* you *become*. Spiritual, scriptural, and wisdom teaching have spoken to the absolute power of the creative mind for millennia. Neuroscience now provides a grounded and scientific understanding of how your brain and neurophysiological system acts as a goal-achieving machine and how your perceptions, emotions, actions, and results are manufactured by what you believe. Together they form a complete understanding of the whole human being operating system. Having a deeper knowledge of this will support you in committing yourself fully to the fact that your entire life is your own creation and that the challenges, experiences, and triumphs are simply an outer objectification of your inner attitude.

Second, you must have a way to *integrate* the understanding into an *actionable* plan—a series of simple step-by-step instructions to transform the way you think. To change your beliefs so that you can transform both your inner and outer realities. Right now you are at the entrance to the doorway. You know what you want (your One Thing) and you've begun to identify the limited beliefs and patterns of thinking that are the *only* things preventing you from creating, being, doing, or achieving your One Thing. These are your Inner Conflicts. Now let's take a next step into understanding how your beliefs really do dictate your destiny and an even deeper look into where your beliefs came from so that you can learn how to transform them, permanently.

6

The Psychology of Beliefs

**"A man is but a product of his thoughts.
What he thinks he becomes."**
—Mahatma Gandhi

B eliefs, once born, will realize themselves into our reality. Not through
some sort of magic fairy dust, but through the precise mechanism
by which we operate as human beings. Small conclusions we come to at
a time we barely remember objectify themselves into nearly every aspect
of our lives. They inform the way we think, the way we react, even the
way we identify with ourselves. They become a part of our personality.
The word, once established, becomes flesh.

On one hand, this is a great thing. Your accomplishments, the things
you cherish most in your life, the aspects of yourself that you are most
proud of, are all a result of empowering beliefs you developed that con-
ceived themselves into your personhood and your life. The fact that beliefs become reality—and a part of you—isn't a problem. On the other
hand, when we are unaware of our *limiting* beliefs or left without tools
to transform them, our lives can feel stuck. To see how your beliefs shape

your reality, and what you can do to change your current circumstances, you must understand the Five Primary Drivers.

The Five Primary Drivers

The Five Primary Drivers illustrate how the beliefs we have inform the results we produce. This notion that what we think drives our outcomes is at the core of behavioral psychology, and it's really common sense. What you believe determines what you think. What you think informs how you feel. How you feel drives your behavior, and your behavior and actions determine the results you do or do not produce, the goals you do or do not achieve, and ultimately the life you either do or do not live. Let's take a look!

The Five Primary Drivers

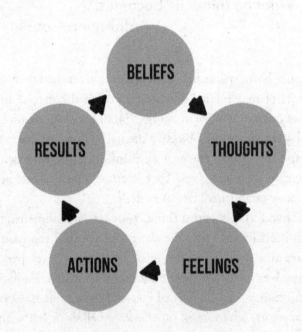

Your Beliefs Dictate Your Thoughts

It shouldn't be surprising that your beliefs dictate your thoughts. If you believe that money is hard to make, you're not likely to access thoughts and ideas of making money easily. If you believe there is no solution to your relationship problem, you won't think about how to solve it. If you believe there's so much that needs to get done and not enough time in your day to do it, then you'll focus your attention toward stress-related thoughts. What you believe, the core "programs" you adopted as a child, inform the way you think now as an adult.

A simple exercise you can do in order to see the impact of your childhood belief systems is to complete a very simple statement: When I was growing up, money was_____. Whatever your answer, there is a high probability that money is that way for you now too. In my experience, about 90 percent of people will relive their parents' experience of life. About 10 percent will rebel against their parents' way and create a transformation. Most people who grew up in an environment where money was scarce and hard to make, or was considered the root of all evil, or was never enough will experience financial insecurity in their lives. A small percentage of folks grow up in financial scarcity and revolt against it—"I'm never going to end up that way"—thus developing a new set of beliefs that lead to financial abundance. Once you learn and implement the tools you'll find in this book, you'll develop the capacity to transform any generational patterns that you've unconsciously adopted.

> ## "The mind is everything. What you think you become."
>
> —Buddha

For years, I knew what I needed to do to take my business to the next level. At that time, that meant I needed to make sales calls. Pretty straightforward. Pick up the phone, make a call, deliver the script. Sometimes I would get a no, other times I'd get the sale. But every time I sat down to

make a sales call, write an email, design a marketing brochure, or do any
other kind of productive activity that might lead to my desired results
(in this case, a sale), it was as if an invisible force was holding me back. If
you could listen to my inner dialogue in those moments, you might have
heard something like, *But I don't know how to do it right. What if I bother
someone? This email isn't very well written. I'm never going to get this right.
The last three calls I made were all no's. I must be doing something wrong.
What am I doing wrong?*

The belief I developed at the age of seven while working on my
school project that "I don't know how to do it right" was unconsciously
shaping my external perception and my internal dialogue at the age of
thirty-three. And it wasn't just in my business that "I don't know how to
do it right" became a core tenant of my thinking; it was in almost every
area of my life. I didn't know how to speak to women. I didn't know how
to make money. I didn't know how to soothe myself without drugs or
alcohol. I didn't know how to lose weight. Something was wrong with
me. I just didn't know *how to do it right*.

Your Thoughts Dictate How You Feel

Your thoughts create neurochemical responses in your body that allow
you to experience the thought as an emotion. In other words, your
thoughts produce feelings. So there I was, sitting in front of my computer,
knowing that the only thing I needed to do in order to generate more
sales and more income was to reach out to potential prospects. But as I
sat there I began to experience "I don't know how to do it right" as if it
was *actually* happening. I began to experience a future that I didn't want
right there in the present moment. Pretty crazy, right? Alone, in front of
my computer, I imagined the rejection of another no. I experienced the
shame of someone hanging up on me. I felt the frustration of another
email unanswered. I was experiencing a future that I would do anything
to avoid sitting right there, in that present moment, before even taking
the first step.

Your Feelings Determine Your Actions

Would you take action to do a thing that you were already experiencing the failure or fear of? Of course you wouldn't. And neither did I. So rather than make sales calls and reach out to potential prospects, I would do anything other than that. We've all developed a unique set of avoidance or procrastination mechanisms. Maybe it's browsing the web or social media. Maybe it's texting a friend or organizing your desk. Maybe, like me, it's heading to Starbucks for a second or third cup of coffee. (Starbucks can feel so comforting, can't it?) People often talk about self-sabotage, not understanding what it is or why they do it. Self-sabotage is simply taking action that's not in alignment with the results you want to produce, and the cause of self-sabotage is a limiting belief, or an Inner Conflict, and the emotional discomfort it manufactures. It's a present-moment fear that what you're wanting to achieve isn't possible, so why bother? It's so simple and straightforward, yet so invisible until we become aware of it.

Your Actions Determine Your Results

Your actions produce the results you have in your life. If action is the cause, the result is the effect. And in my case, instead of a highly productive business, my result was a highly caffeinated David.

I was spending so much time drifting and distracting myself from the things I knew I needed to do that I started feeling even worse about myself. *Why can't I just commit to do the things I said I'm going to do? I'm not very disciplined. What's wrong with me? Why does it feel so difficult to sit there and just get the work done? I'm never going to figure this out. I should be further along than this by now.* In observation of my own behavior, I came to the same conclusion I started with: that I just didn't know how to do it right.

Your Results Reinforce Your Beliefs

When you step back and look at the results you are producing, you will notice an illuminating thing: your actions always, without question, reinforce the original beliefs you started with.

Six months and only a few sales later, I analyzed my own results and concluded that I just didn't know how to do sales calls. I supposed I wasn't disciplined enough. I just wasn't a very good salesperson and decided that this job simply wasn't for me. Perhaps I was too introverted. Maybe the leads were no good. The sales script ineffective. Or perhaps I just wasn't "cut out" for it. Through the experience, I reinforced my own limiting beliefs and self-perception and deepened the false narrative that "I don't know how to do it right" all as a result of a failure to understand that none of these things were actually true. The only truth was that I was operating according to a subconscious program named "I don't know how to do it right," and without intervention that program would play out precisely as it had my entire life.

The Five Primary Drivers are a self-fulfilling prophecy: *What you believe, you think. What you think, you feel. What you feel, you act upon. How you act determines your results (or lack thereof). And your results always, 100 percent of the time, reinforce the original belief.*

The mistake that most people make in trying to change their life is that they attempt to modify their *actions*. Try a different weight-loss program. Pursue a different marketing strategy. Hope that the next date brings a completely different partner. We end up going round and round and round on some sort of action-oriented carousel looking for the next magic pill or strategy or hoping that this time our actions will produce different results. But the lynchpin, the mechanism that changes the entire dynamic of your life, are your beliefs. Change your beliefs and you change the results.

Your Brain Is a Goal-Achieving Machine

If you and I were to sit together for a few hours and have a casual conversation, I could tell you things about your life that under ordinary circumstances I should never know. How much money you make, what kind of relationship you have, how you feel about your life, whether it's stressful or relaxed, a great likelihood of being able to identify if you have any health problems, what kind of relationship you have with your parents or your children. Conversely, if I were to secretly follow you for a few days and observe your daily life, what you do, take a look at how much you make, see what kind of relationships you're in, evaluate your health, I could tell you precisely what you believe.

Back when I used to do one-day intensives with private clients, I would start out by just letting them talk to me about their lives. By listening to their stories, it was clear to me what they believed. One client of mine, Jennifer, struggled to grow her business for over two years and talked about her business as having "been in a drought." Another client, Nina, was highly successful in business but had been single for over a decade and loved what she called "the bad boy type" but complained that "they always cheated" and "could never be trusted." A former Olympic gold medalist that I coached, Alex, was having a difficult time building his fitness training company because he believed that after the Olympics there wasn't anything he was going to be "as successful at" as the games.

None of these beliefs were necessarily true. They were just ideas. But ideas are alive. And given enough time and energy and trajectory, a belief is 100 percent destined to objectify itself into your reality. Change their trajectory and you change the direction of your future.

I helped Jennifer see that her business wasn't in a drought but in a healthy, productive, and very much-needed period of reorganization. Within six months, she was generating more revenue more easily than ever before.

Nina actually loved dynamic, outgoing men, and there were plenty of them out there who weren't unfaithful or dishonest. Within a year, she met the man she's now happily married to.

Alex had the skill, discipline, and work ethic to be as successful, if not more successful, in his new fitness training company as he had been as an Olympic athlete. He now runs a highly successful training and fitness company.

But until we were able to identify the limiting beliefs, or Inner Conflicts, that each of them had been carrying for most of their lives and transform those limiting beliefs into empowered beliefs that were in alignment with the results they wanted to produce, it was nearly impossible for my clients to change their circumstances or results.

No matter how many new client strategies Jennifer attempted...

No matter how many men Nina dated...

No matter what Alex did in his fitness training business...

None of them had the capacity to produce different results until they worked with the *actual* cause of all their current results: their beliefs.

Beliefs are the lynchpin to transformation. Most people fail to appreciate the profound impact that beliefs have on their daily lives. Not just the thoughts that you have but the feelings you feel and the way you perceive your circumstances and experiences. Even the daily decisions you make. The videos you watch, the way you have conversations, the restaurants you select, the seat you choose and who you sit next to, the time you decide to leave the house or make the sales call, or the clothes you choose to put on today are all driven by beliefs and thoughts that have an influence on whether you will produce the desired results you have in any area of your life or whether you will continue to experience the absence of those results. Think about it. These seemingly random choices create the entire container within which your reality exists. But they are all driven by one thing—your core beliefs.

Your Beliefs Dictate Your Destiny

One of my clients was frustrated that she continued to meet prospective clients who expressed an initial interest in working with her but inevitably either didn't have the resources to afford her services or would disappear and become nonresponsive just as the sale was about to be closed.

"It must be that I'm targeting the wrong person or there's a problem with my marketing or messaging," she said. "Maybe I have an issue with my sales skills. Something is definitely off!"

She was right. Something *was* off. Her beliefs. Her fear that what she offered may not be valuable enough or that prospects would scoff at her pricing. Her fear that she would never have enough money. Her fear around her worthiness. Ultimately what we discovered was that at some level she believed that nobody would want to do business with her.

These beliefs were informing all kinds of seemingly insignificant decisions that were attracting and connecting her to prospects who would materialize her limiting beliefs and fears into the reality of her experiences. The woman who she struck up a conversation with at the business networking event, the company that contacted her via her website, the referral she got from one of her past clients (all of whom she failed to enroll as clients) are all connected to a sophisticated invisible structure of unconscious choices and decisions that she (and they) are making in order to orchestrate the experience that "nobody wants to do business with her." We are all operating within one infinitely intelligent system that is interacting with itself and with us to align an entire network of individuals, circumstances, situations, and beliefs toward the production of highly predictable outcomes. Instead of looking within to identify the psychological cause that was the driving force of her experience, she was looking outside herself to explain why it was happening and how to fix it.

"How did you meet the woman at the networking event?" I asked her.

"She and I were the first two to arrive at the meeting, and we had a mutual friend in common. We hit it off immediately, and I was sure that she was going to be interested in us working together based on what she said she needed and how perfect a fit she was for our services."

"And when she told you she might be interested in working with you, what did you think?" I asked.

She paused for a moment. "I thought, 'Wow, finally someone who wants to work with me. Maybe this one will finally come through.'"

"What do you mean by 'finally come through'?" I asked.

"Well, it had been so many clients one after another that didn't pan out," she said, "that I started to feel…desperate. I actually started to worry I was never going to get another client or at least afraid it might take so long that it would put me in real financial pressure."

"Got it. So when you met this woman you were in a state of feeling like you were never going to get another client?" I asked.

She paused for a moment. I could see she was starting to connect the dots and that she was moving into a new level of understanding and integration.

"Oh my God!" she laughed. "Of course I had to show up early, and she did too, so that we could connect and have a conversation that led me to believe she was interested in working together only to have the same experience of a prospect bailing on me again. It's a self-fulfilling prophecy, isn't it?"

"Yep," I said. "The good news is now that you understand it's not anything external, like your sales skills or your messaging or bad luck, that's producing the undesired result, we can work on shifting the one thing that's causing this repetitive experience for you—your belief. Change your belief and you change your outcomes."

You don't have to believe in a "law of attraction" or "magic of the universe" to understand how every single result you do or do not create in any aspect of your life is a result of your beliefs. It's literally how the human being operating system works. The psychological sciences explain quite clearly that your brain is a goal-achieving machine, and the instructions it is operating against are the assumptions or beliefs you have about life. Your beliefs are informing your conscious and unconscious mind and are bringing forth into your reality exactly what it is that you believe. Without much force, you can radically transform your external reality when you adjust your inner architecture or attitude. But if you truly want to transform your life, you must become 100 percent committed, faithful, and loyal to the idea that *you* are creating the experiences of your life by the design of your own thinking. You must become what I call "radically responsible." You must accept that every single experience you are (or are not) having is a direct result of what you believe. There are no exceptions.

The moment you attribute an explanation to a force outside yourself, you create a precedent where some things are within your control and others are not. Sure, the economy may be bad, but some people are thriving. Yes, the prognosis may not be good, but some people recover from it. Okay, the relationship may have challenges, but other couples are able to re-create their passion. The moment you give power to a cause outside your beliefs, you lose the power to change your circumstances. There isn't anything in your life that you cannot transform by changing your beliefs about it. In fact, there is no force more powerful in the world than a changed mind. When you commit to radical responsibility, and you have a framework for transforming your limiting beliefs, and you stay loyal to that practice on a moment-by-moment basis, any change you can imagine becomes possible.

In the next chapter, I'm going to teach you the neuroscience of beliefs: where they're actually stored, how to access them, and how to begin to change them. But before we jump into that, it may be helpful to do a quick inventory of your limiting beliefs.

Over the last decade I've cataloged over a thousand limiting beliefs that people have. That may sound like a lot, but there are less than a hundred that comprise the most common limiting beliefs. And only a few dozen that are at the core of all our suffering. I invite you to take just a few minutes to go through the Limiting Beliefs Checklist I've put together online and see which of the beliefs on the list resonate with you. If they feel familiar, that means the resonance, or energy of the belief, is inside you and something that you'll likely want to address with the tools from this book.

It's certainly possible to have empowering and limiting beliefs about the same subject. For example, some days you feel you're good enough but other days you feel like you're not good enough. That's normal. The work we're going to be doing throughout the rest of this journey is to pull the weeds of those limiting beliefs out so they no longer hold you back from your goals, vision, and full potential. Doing a quick inventory of your psychological warehouse will be invaluable as we move forward, because you'll want an awareness of your biggest limiting beliefs as we do this work together.

Once you finish with your reading today, visit www.DavidBayer. com/checklist and take just five minutes to go through the quick checklist. You may be surprised at what you find! In the next chapter, I'll give you even more context around what your limiting beliefs really are and why they can seem so elusive, even when you're committed to your personal growth potential.

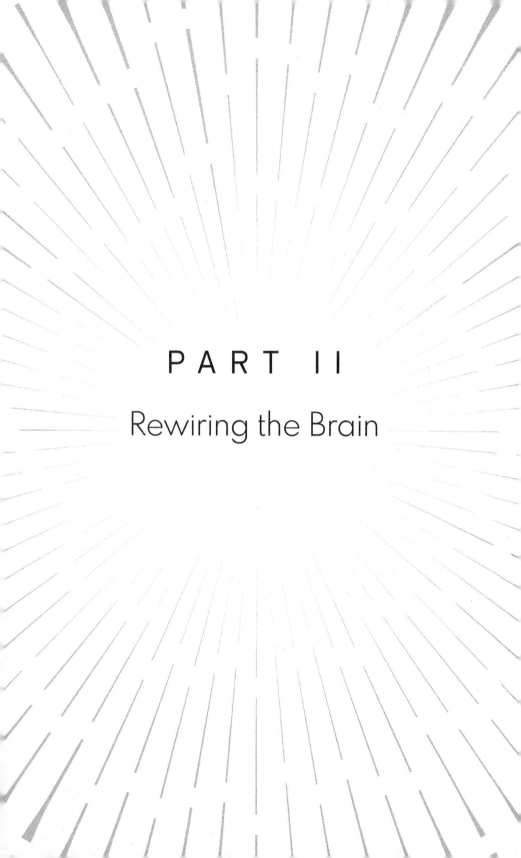

PART II

Rewiring the Brain

7

The Neuroscience of Transformation

You are born with approximately one hundred billion neurons in your brain. Neurons are a specific type of cell that use electrical impulses and chemical signals to transmit information between different areas of the brain and between the brain and the rest of the nervous system. You're also born with approximately twenty-five billion synaptic connections. Synapses are like little bridges that connect neurons to each other and to the rest of the body. You can think of this network of neurons and synaptic connections as a neurophysiological matrix that underpins many aspects of your psychological and emotional experience of life, including your memories, inner talk, perceptions, and belief systems.

If you do the math, you'll notice that you are born with more neurons than connections. Meaning, not all neurons are connected yet into the mainframe of your brain or body. So which ones are?

Well, nature has a highly intelligent way of operating. At birth, your consciousness has already been transmitted into a hardware that came fully equipped with the necessary features and functions to give you life and keep you alive. Contained within your newborn bodysuit and wired up in the circuitry are the primary survival functions: eating, pooping, crying, seeing, breathing, sensing, moving. Everything you need in order to sustain life is already wired into the system. So what about those other seventy-five billion neurons that aren't yet connected and programmed?

In nature's infinite wisdom, what was also included in the default operating system was a blank canvas. A space to create uniqueness and our own individual identity and personhood. An infinite potential of perceptions, beliefs, experiences, and biases that would shape each and every one of our personalities and destinies differently. By the age of seven, the average human brain has gone from one hundred billion neurons and twenty-five billion synaptic connections to the same number of neurons with over a quadrillion (a thousand trillion) connections. So what happened? Well, life happened.

From the day you came into the world, you've been recording your experiences into the hard drive and wiring of your brain. Every single moment of your existence has been captured. Your five senses—sight, taste, touch, sound, and smell—have been ingesting the data of your daily experiences, sending it through the nervous system, where it is organized in the brain and compiled into a variety of outputs, including memories. New connections form between neurons as new memories are created.

The first time you experienced a dog, you saw the dog, heard the dog, smelled the dog, touched the dog, and maybe, if your parents weren't keeping a close eye on you, grabbed your first little taste of dog fur. All of that information was sent through your nervous system to your brain, where a memory of that experience was compiled. But in addition to the sensory data, another piece of data was unconsciously input into the database related to this experience with the dog: the meaning you gave the experience with the dog.

If your experience was pleasurable and you enjoyed the feeling of your fluffy furry friend and the wet licks on your hands and face and felt safe and comfortable in the situation, then you may have given a meaning to the experience that "dogs are friendly" or fun or your new best friend. If, however, you perceived the experience as unfriendly or first experienced an overly rambunctious dog or a dog that doesn't do well with children or, in extreme cases, if you were attacked or bitten by a dog, you would record the data involved with that experience along with the applied meaning that "dogs are dangerous."

This initial dog interaction and the meaning or belief you gave to the experience becomes the foundation of each subsequent experience you have that seems similar to the original. The next time you interacted with a dog, the brain, in an effort to assess the new experience as quickly as possible and determine whether there was an immediate threat or pleasure opportunity, used the database of past experiences you had to match, as best as it could, the new experience with a prior one. What it also did, at a rate so rapid that it bypasses the conscious thought process, was to apply the same meaning to the new experience that was applied to the prior one. You experienced this meaning in the form of a thought. And regardless of whether the new interaction was with a completely different dog, you would have had the same reaction, that *dogs are friendly* or *dogs are dangerous*, that you had in your original experience. A lens was created that, left to its own devices, would continue to influence each subsequent experience with every dog.

The Story You Tell Yourself

At a New Year's Eve party several years ago, my wife and I arrived early at the hosts' house and greeted the other guests as they arrived. One of our friends, a 6'4", 235-pound boulder of a man, arrived a few minutes after we did. The host had a happy, yappy 5-pound Chihuahua that let guests know through his incessant barking that he was the top dog in the house. Our giant friend took one look at the little dog and, without hesitation, began screaming, "Does he bite? Does he bite?" as he jumped up on the sofa to escape the tiny canine harmlessly posturing for attention. In a later conversation with our friend, we uncovered that, as a three-year old, he was bitten by a neighbor's dog. Ever since then, anytime he has encountered another dog, without thinking, he panics. He shared that he's even aware that his reaction doesn't make any sense most of the time, but he can't help it. It's simply an automatic response. His belief that "dogs are dangerous" invokes a threat response (fear) that instinctively drives his actions. It's simply the way the operating system works. You can't outwit or outwork your beliefs. But you *can* change them.

Your beliefs are stored in the neural networks of your brain. Every experience you've ever had is locked away in a vast storage vault of quadrillions upon quadrillions of data points that hold the key to your unique perception of life and everything in it. Each memory has embedded with it the meaning you gave the experience, and these memories combine to create a highly complex and unique lens through which you're experiencing the world. The moment you have an experience, your brain searches the vast constellation of information inside you, presents a meaning from a similar prior experience, and you live the new moment through the lens of the originating meaning or belief. You bring the knowledge of the past into your present moment in order to ensure your survival of it.

In many ways this is a highly useful feature of the operating system. You can imagine how difficult it would have been for early humans to survive without memory. Once attacked by a saber-toothed tiger, one would want to retain the memory of that experience to give a head start on avoiding the next one. Imagine as a child learning the importance of looking both ways before crossing the street, only to forget that critical instruction the next time. We wouldn't last very long without the ability to interpret the new moment with some information gained from the prior experience—without the capacity to remember. In each new experience your brain is data matching with a past memory and applying the same meaning that you invented the first time around. But that's where things get a little sticky.

The new moment isn't the old moment. In fact, no two experiences are the same. Each new moment affords a new experience and a new opportunity. This new dog isn't the same as that old dog. This new relationship isn't the same as that old relationship. This new business opportunity isn't the same as that last one. But that's how we experience them. To make matters more complex, in each new moment we experience an inner dialogue that is aligned with the original experience. We literally hear a voice in our head that says, *Watch out! That dog is dangerous*, or *This is never going to work out for me*, or *Why do people always show such lack of consideration*, or *What am I doing wrong?*

The complicated part about all of this is that the inner dialogue, or what I like to call "the story" that you tell yourself, sounds and feels as if it's actually you. It's told in what seems to be your inner voice. If we were to determine a location for it, we would say it comes from inside you, most likely from your head space. It *seems* like you are talking to yourself. Except you're not.

The story you hear is an unconsciously generated dialogue or "tape" that automatically runs based on the story you told yourself the first time an experience like this happened. You then react instinctively to the story, without questioning the validity of it and, as in the case of our dog-fearing friend, go from zero to panic in an instant.

Seeing the Story as a Story

My first profound experience of this was in the early stages of my journey into personal development. I was driving to work one day, and my route required a brief ten-minute stint on the highway. As I was only a few exits away from my office, I decided to drive in the slow lane. All of a sudden a speeding truck hurled down the on-ramp next to me, entered the highway, and cut me off, nearly causing an accident. I was startled to say the least, and in my shock and fright I immediately began thinking to myself, *I can't believe that guy. Who does he think he is? Didn't he see me here? I'll show him!*

I punched my fist toward the center of my steering wheel ready to slam on my horn, and in a moment of realization it hit me. None of what I was telling myself was true. In all likelihood the guy in the truck didn't see me. He didn't know me. Nothing was personal. It wasn't a matter of respect. It wasn't any of the things that I was telling myself. In fact as I saw the story and realized that none of it was true, I relaxed and moved into appreciation. Grateful that I was paying attention. Feeling fortunate that I was able to slow my car down and avoid an accident. Calmed by the fact that this really had nothing to do with me and everything to do with another driver who simply wasn't paying their best attention. And in that calm and gratitude, I actually wished the other driver well and said a little prayer for both of us that we would be protected and safe in our travels. The moment I was able to see the story for what it was, an untrue narrative based on my habitual beliefs and thoughts and emotions and actions, it opened up a space for a new way of interpreting the experience.

While viewing the present moment through the lens of the past is a critical neurocognitive feature supporting survival, it isn't conducive to having a joyful or powerful experience of life, achieving your full potential, or catalyzing change. In fact it's conducive to what I call a "groundhog day" type of existence, named after the classic Bill Murray comedy. In that film, Murray's character wakes up and experiences the same day over and over again. He's trapped in a single day filled with the same experiences. Over time, it drives him mad. In an attempt to escape the crazy-making cycle of living the same day over and over again, he begins to invent creative ways to kill himself, including the classic scene where he's kidnapped the local town celebrity groundhog, Punxsutawney Phil, and drives his car headfirst into a speeding oncoming train. The movie is quite funny, but the reality that most people are living a groundhog day type of existence is anything but.

Left to our own operating system, we too will experience each new experience the same way—through the lens of our limiting beliefs and "the story" we've told ourselves, over and over again, despite the fact that each new experience is, well, new. A new dog, a new relationship, a new business opportunity, a new job, a new possibility. Each moment is unique. But until we learn how to consciously manage our reactions, interpretations, and belief systems, we are destined to live the same quality of life over and over again. Different relationship, but same relationship. Different conflict, but same reaction. Different job, but same dissatisfaction. Different health problem, but still health problems. Different car ride, but same road rage. In a very real and profound way, until we are able to see that our beliefs are shaping our perception of the present moment in ways that don't actually reflect the reality of the new moment, and until we see the story for the story, we aren't actually living in the present moment but a distorted version of the present moment shaped by our experiences and beliefs and memories from the past. We're living the same experience over and over again, despite the fact that life is presenting a new opportunity, a possibility for change.

The Brain Is a Storyteller

It's important to realize that most of the time we aren't consciously thinking. The vast majority of each and every day we are habitually reacting to new experiences as if they were old experiences. The brain is serving one of its primary functions, which is to ensure our survival, and on a moment-by-moment basis it's manufacturing a sophisticated narrative, or a story, that matches up with the beliefs we have about ourselves and every aspect of our lives. The brain is a storyteller. And your thoughts, for the most part, are not your thoughts but simply unconscious psychological habits. Just as your heart beats and your lungs breathe, so too does your brain produce thoughts whether you're actively engaged with the thinking process or not. If you want to free yourself from your psychological and emotional habits so you can create an opportunity for something new in your life, it's important to understand the machinery at work so you can elevate yourself to be a master of the machinery rather than continue to participate as a helpless passenger continuing down the same unfulfilling road when there are so many possible routes on the rich road map of your life.

I invite you to put this book down for a moment. To sit comfortably in your chair or upright in your bed or wherever you are. To take a few deep breaths to relax your body and to spend just one minute with your eyes closed. And while you do that, try not to think. Go ahead. What you'll notice, and why so many people who begin to meditate or engage in a mindfulness practice have such a challenge, is that you can't *not* think. Your brain has become so habituated to thinking as a mechanism for survival that even when you are sitting with your eyes closed in an environment with no external stimulation, it will bring up thoughts or memories or ideas for it to think about. What do we think about this? What do we think about that? Before you know it you're off following some thought train that has nothing to do with anything relevant to your day. The brain is addicted to the process of thinking. And that in and of itself isn't necessarily a problem. The problem arises when you do not realize that your thoughts are not your thoughts, and you fail to distinguish between what you actually think about the present moment and the brain's unconscious opinion or story about it.

> **"The brain does not think but serves as the interpretation of stimuli which cause thought."**
> —Napoleon Hill

Similar to how the Five Primary Drivers work—where your beliefs inform your thoughts, your thoughts inform your emotions, your emotions inform your actions, your actions inform your results, and your results reinforce the originating belief—so too does the story you tell yourself inform how you feel and, from there, what you do and the results you produce. From a psychological perspective, your beliefs dictate your destiny. And from a neuroscientific perspective, the quality of your life is equal to the quality of the story you tell yourself. Until you have the tools to consciously insert yourself into the process, by questioning the story, you become trapped in what's called a psycho-cybernetic loop. You bring past beliefs into your present moment as you relive the past again in the here and now. You reinforce those beliefs at an even deeper level and become even more likely to tell yourself the same story the next time around. You accumulate so much evidence for the story that it becomes hardwired into your reality.

Use Your Mind to Change Your Brain

Up until the late 1800s, scientists believed that the brain was fixed or hardwired. In other words, the way you thought and perceived was something that was fixed within your personality and there was no way to actually change who you were. It was as if some sort of karmic die was cast just before your birth and the brain you got was the brain you were stuck with. In early studies, most people's brains did seem to stay the same—in part because what you think determines your results, and your results simply reinforce what you think.

But in 1890, William James, considered by many as the father of modern psychology, proposed a theory that the brain could change, that it was malleable and capable of reorganizing. Decades later his theory proved to be true when neuroscientists discovered that stroke victims who had damaged parts of their brain were able to use cognitive therapy and other techniques to relearn behavior that was lost due to the brain damage and observed that those corresponding parts of the brain regrew. The discovery was groundbreaking: you can use your mind to actually change your brain.

This idea is at the core of Personal Development 2.0 and is part of the fundamental definition of what mindset is. Mindset is the developed capacity to use your mind to change your brain, and it is the single most important skill you must learn if you want to achieve your full potential and live an extraordinary life. The doorway to this transformation begins the moment you see the story as a story. When you see the story as a story, you are now *seeing* the story rather than *being* the story. The moment you see the story, you are now aware of the machinery rather than being an unwilling participant in it. It is in the seeing of the story that you open up a small but critical space to begin to question your interpretation of the present moment, which is also a questioning of your beliefs and, in a great sense, a questioning of the entire way you've been viewing life for your entire life. It is in this magical, transformative moment that you now have a choice, and that choice is the key to creating a dramatic shift in your current reality and life.

Mindset is the developed capacity to use your mind to change your brain.

The Story vs. What Happened

When I was transitioning away from my career in search engine optimization and before I had any sense that my teachings on personal development would actually turn into a career, my wife Carol encouraged me to begin sharing what I was learning about transformation. Based on that encouragement, she and I rented a small classroom at Rollins College in Winter Park, Florida. I invited friends and acquaintances to join me for a one-day presentation where I shared the early versions of my framework and methodologies on how to create a changed mind and a changed life. Twenty-three people showed up that Saturday, including four teenagers: two boys and two girls.

After I taught on the neuroscience of transformation, I had each participant take a moment to think about a recent situation or experience, similar to my story about the driver who "cut me off," where they reacted in a way that was emotionally charged or distressed. I asked them to write out the story with all of the charged, emotional, limiting-belief-driven language they could remember—to capture the anger or sadness or jealousy or frustration and to document as best they could the story that the brain was telling. Then I asked them to rewrite the experience simply through the lens of what I call "What Happened." To write out the experience expressing only the facts about what happened without the belief-driven narrative, without the story.

Now that they could see the story separated from the actual experience, I next asked them to see if there was a reinterpretation of the event that might be possible, that could be more in alignment with what they wanted, and encouraged them to look for the gift, the blessing, or the opportunity in the actual experience. I then asked if anyone wanted to share what they found.

One of the teenage girls, Madison, who was dating one of the teenage boys in attendance, C. J., raised her hand. She had a look of concern on her face, and it was clear that something had shaken her. I asked her what she had discovered, and she shared in front of the group.

"Do you remember when everyone was doing the ALS ice bucket challenge? People were pouring ice-cold buckets of water on their heads to raise money to find a cure for Lou Gehrig's disease?" she asked. I nodded. "Well, C. J. wouldn't do it. Everybody else was doing it, but he refused. And I thought to myself, 'Why won't he do it? Everybody else is doing it. He's no fun. He's such a drag. Is this how he's always going to be? I don't want to be with someone that doesn't want to have fun,'" she said.

"So over the last few weeks it's been bothering me. I've started to take note of everything he does that is an indicator that he doesn't like to have fun. I think I've even been imagining some of these things. And I've been seriously entertaining the idea that maybe he's not the right person for me. That I'm going to grow old into a boring life with him. In fact I had planned on talking to him and telling him that I thought maybe we should take a break."

She began crying. "Why are you crying?" I asked.

"Because I love C. J. The whole thing was made up in my mind. When you asked me to write down just 'what happened,' the truth was simply that I asked him if he wanted to do the ice bucket challenge and he said no and when I asked him why not he said, 'Because I'm just not interested in it.' That was it. And everything else was just a story."

C. J. looked up at Madison as she continued to share. I could only imagine what story was going on in his head as he was just informed that he was on the brink of being dumped by his beloved girlfriend for refusing to pour a bucket of water on his head.

"Was there anything else you realized?" I asked.

"Yeah," she said. "I realized that this is what I did to the last two guys I dated. They didn't want to do something I wanted to do, and I created this story that they were boring and they weren't going to be any fun. And I realized I've done this with girlfriends too. And none of it has ever been true. I've just been scared that I was going to make a wrong decision and be stuck for the rest of my life with something that I didn't want, and as I'm saying it now it sounds so crazy."

"Where do you think you came up with this story?" I asked.

"It's so obvious," she said. "From seeing my parents get divorced. It was hard. I saw how much pain they both went through, and I swore I would never go through that kind of pain myself. So I'm super hypercritical of people around me because I'm afraid of getting into a relationship that doesn't work out and going through all that pain."

The feeling of breakthrough was palpable in the room as Madison continued to steamroll through her limiting beliefs and her current story. "And I realized what's really true is that I love C. J. I love how independent he is. I love that he doesn't just go along with everyone else. I love that he's not afraid to stand up for himself and to do things differently." Madison began to cry again and turned to look at C. J. for the first time.

"Why is this so upsetting to you, Madison?" I asked.

"Because I was about to change my entire life over a story that was never true in the first place," she sobbed. C. J. stood up to give her a hug and the two embraced as the adults in the room, many of whom were also sobbing, smiled in admiration.

Our limiting beliefs and stories cause us to perpetuate lives that aren't ours to live. They cause harm to others. They create blame, jealousy, anger, insecurity, and suffering. They are the cause of arguments, breakups, and divorces. They are what keep us stuck in poverty, depression, a job we don't love, a relationship without passion. They are the singular cause of stress, disease, disagreement, and even war. The quality of our stories dictates the quality of our lives. When we see the story as just that—a story—we create an opportunity to change the beliefs we've been carrying with us for years, often decades, and in an instant create a profoundly changed future. At the core of all transformation is a new belief, and a new belief creates a changed mind. The question then is, How do you permanently change your beliefs?

8

The Power of Decision

It was Christmas Day and I was sitting at home alone. I had plans to head over to a friend's house for dinner but had nothing scheduled for the day, so I decided to get a head start on my new-year goal setting. It was 2012. I had been single for almost a decade. Most of that time had been spent in frustration and deep in my porn addiction. There were many times when I felt like giving up entirely, certain that I would be alone for the rest of my life. I was plagued by limiting beliefs, by old patterns of thought.

I had managed to get two years of sobriety under my belt and felt like I was ready to be in a new relationship. I sat in front of my computer and started grabbing a variety of images and pasting them onto my digital vision board. A dream house on an island. A picture of a public speaker speaking in front of thousands of people. A man at a book signing. A picture of someone doing yoga representing my own health and spiritual wellness. I thought about what kind of woman I wanted to be with. Someone who was intelligent, spiritual, kind, loving, compassionate. I went through the list of qualities that I was looking for and then moved on to the physical. Long dark hair. Beautiful olive skin. In that moment I thought to myself, *I'm going to meet a beautiful Colombian woman and make her my wife.* I don't know why I picked a Colombian woman. It might have been because some of the most beautiful women I had ever

71

met were Colombian. It was, in a sense, a random and somewhat uncharacteristic thought. But regardless, it's what I had decided. I didn't know when, I didn't know how, but soon I was going to meet the woman of my dreams.

I was living in Orlando, Florida, at the time. Each week I'd make the two-hour drive to Sarasota to work with a naturopathic doctor that a friend had recommended. A few months prior I had torn my left rotator cuff for the second time and wanted to see if there was a way to naturally heal my shoulder and avoid surgery. So each week I'd meet up with Dr. Zane for a series of muscle injections, acupuncture, and massage to repair my shoulder. Zane's birthday was the first week in January, so that weekend I decided to stay overnight and take him out to dinner. He recommended a restaurant near his home, and at around 8:00 p.m. we headed out for dinner. Turned out the restaurant was a local hot spot and required a reservation, so Zane and I had about an hour wait ahead of us. Seeing as we were both nondrinkers, we sidled on up to the bar to grab a couple of nonalcoholic beverages. I had noticed a group of three beautiful women when we arrived at the restaurant who were busy chatting away on the other side of the bar. Zane noticed me noticing them.

"I get so uncomfortable hanging out in places like this," he said.

"Why?" I asked.

"Well, I'm just not that good at talking to women, so every time I'm in a place like this I'm torn between this desire to go over and say hello and the fear that they're just going to reject me."

I could totally relate to Zane. I had been terrified of approaching women my entire life. Some people say their greatest fear is public speaking. Maybe. But mine was approaching a beautiful stranger and saying hello. For whatever reason Zane's vulnerability was inspiring and gave me the courage to do what would have ordinarily been unthinkable for me.

"Oh, come on," I said, grabbing Zane by the wrist. "It's not that hard."

We made our way over to the three women at the bar. One of them in particular caught my eye. She had long black hair, beautiful olive skin.

I managed to interrupt their conversation just long enough to get in a quick introduction, and apparently that was all I needed.

"Hi, ladies, how are you all doing? My name is David. This is Zane. Where are you all from?"

Carol looked at me with a sideways glance and a subtle grin.

"Colombia," she replied.

Seven years later Carol was my wife.

From one decision: that I was going to meet a beautiful Colombian woman and make her my wife.

Changing Your Beliefs

Most people get stuck in personal development at a very specific point: the actual changing of their beliefs. In the progression of your personal growth you go through a variety of stages. The first stage is a total lack of awareness. You believe the external world is chaotic and unpredictable and that joy, change, accomplishment, and success depend upon a lining up of circumstances that produce those desired results. Luck, in effect, seems to be the determining factor between the happy and the unhappy.

The second stage occurs when one is first exposed to spiritual and self-help distinctions and concepts. You realize that your external reality isn't random but an actualized reflection of your inner architecture and belief systems. You may not be particularly aware of your limiting beliefs, but you know that they're there and they are unconsciously informing the decisions you make and the coincidences and synchronicities that are occurring in your life.

The goal from the second stage of personal growth is to move into the third stage, which is hallmarked by increased self-awareness. You gain greater insights into what you actually think and believe. You begin to tune into the inner dialogue and are able to realize that the little voice in your head isn't actually you but a preprogrammed automatic response to the experiences of your life. You still have the same brain; you're just acutely aware that it isn't programmed in alignment with the life or business or relationships you want. This awareness is accompanied by an intensification of dissatisfaction, frustrations, stress, overwhelm, and generalized suffering. This is where most people stop and why so many are frustrated and feeling unfulfilled and incomplete in their personal growth journey.

This gap—between Personal Development 1.0 and Personal Development 2.0—is hallmarked by an intellectual understanding of personal growth concepts and philosophies yet void of the actual transformation itself. It is in this gap that the vast majority of seekers, including myself, get stuck. No one needed to convince me that my beliefs were holding me back, but I didn't have a strategy or practice for actually changing them, for rewiring my own brain. I refer to this phase of development as "self-awareness purgatory" where you've become acutely aware of your limiting beliefs but don't know how to replace them. It's a painful and uncomfortable phase of the process and is often where people get so frustrated with personal growth that they either become entrenched in a life-long addiction of trying to discover how to "fix" themselves or they just flat out give up.

At various points I was a part of both groups, exhausted from going from event to event, tired of reading the next self-help or spirituality book, dismayed that my meditation practice wasn't seeming to quiet the incessant inner negative chatter, and frustrated that each new transformational process du jour fell short of a meaningful change in my mind. At the same time, I was still in deep contemplation, praying to my higher power, God, to show me the way out of suffering and help me discover how I could go *beyond* personal development and *actually* change the way I thought.

The reason why most people get stuck here is because beliefs seem somewhat intangible. We aren't sure how to grasp them, so we can't change them. They're almost like clouds, so we have a difficult time wrapping our hands and minds around them. So how do you get ahold of them?

Well, the first step is to get clear on what we've established thus far in this book—that beliefs aren't in fact nebulous but are actually clusters of neural synaptic connections, memories, and meanings that are stored within the wiring of our brain. We know they are there. They are real. They are physical. Once you understand that, you can then apply tools and practices to change them. How do you change your limiting beliefs and forge new neural pathways for new and empowered ones and move on to real transformation? By discovering what a limiting belief *really* is.

Beliefs Are Decisions

It was Sunday afternoon, and I was taking a long walk on a beautiful day on Siesta Key beach in Sarasota. As I mentioned, I had been obsessing about this question for weeks, tuning my attention toward the frequency of an answer, when it hit me. So simple that I almost dismissed the distinction, but so powerful that it unlocked an entire new level of access to my own mind and has now transformed the beliefs and lives of tens of thousands of people. What was this mind-changing new awareness?

It was this: *beliefs are decisions.*

Read that again. Beliefs are actually *decisions*. When I was working on the school project in the garage and came to the conclusion that "I didn't know how to do things right," I had actually, unconsciously *decided* that I didn't know how to do things right. It wasn't necessarily true (in fact now having done the work around it I can clearly see that it wasn't), but in that moment and in each and every subsequent experience that seemed like I didn't know how to do it right, I was continuing to make the same decision over and over again. The challenge, of course, is that we don't even remember making these decisions the first time around, and when we made the decisions they weren't conscious decisions but nearly instantaneous, automatic meanings that we gave to the experiences of our lives and to ourselves.

To *decide* means "to cut off all else other than that which you have decided," and that's precisely what you experienced as you were giving meaning to the experiences of your life, creating your belief systems, and building out the structure of your brain. You cut off all possibility of seeing anything other than that which supported the original belief, which then reinforced that belief over and over again until the belief became your solid truth. But by acknowledging this fact, that the only reason you have so much evidence for the belief is because that's what you've paid attention to, and realizing that beliefs are decisions, you create an opportunity for a radical transformation in your thinking, your identity, your view of the world, and the reality of your life.

When you become aware that beliefs are decisions, you gain the ability to change the belief. You have what I call a "response-ability," an ability to respond. Once you realize you've been holding on to a belief that doesn't serve you well, that doesn't feel good when you think it, that isn't in alignment with what you're wanting to create in any area of your life or in your view of yourself, you have a response-ability to take one simple but powerful action.

You make a new decision.

You may feel like you don't know how to change your beliefs. But you certainly know how to make new decisions. At some point in your life you *decided* you wanted to date someone, you dated them, then you *decided* you no longer wanted to date them. You *decided* you were interested in a particular type of career or position, you acquired the position, and then you *decided* you no longer wanted the position. You *decided* that you wanted to grow personally or spiritually, you grew spiritually and personally, and then *decided* that you wanted to go beyond your current state of personal growth and, well, here we are. Your life is the sum of all the decisions you've made about life, and the actions you took or didn't take from those decisions, and the corresponding results you produced as a result of those actions. Beliefs are decisions. And when you decide something *different* about yourself or your life—that money is easy to make, that you can reinvigorate your health, that there's enough time to get the important things done, that life is conspiring to bring you the resources you need—those decisions *realize* themselves into your reality.

Want to change your reality? Make a new decision. It's really that simple.

Can I Really Just Decide?

You may be asking, *Can I really just make a new decision?* I appreciate the question. It seems too simple, doesn't it? After all, what we've been led to believe is that transformation is difficult, that it takes a long time, perhaps years of therapy, that old traumas are hard to resolve and heal. And truth be told if you've been on your own journey of personal growth for some time like I have, you've probably accumulated evidence to support those limiting ideas. I can only share with you my experience and the experience of the thousands of people who have been willing to try on what I'm sharing with you in this book. It doesn't have to be that difficult, and yes, you can simply make a new decision. The honest truth is that you just sort of made a random decision the first time around, but because of the way the human being operating system works, it kept reinforcing itself over and over again.

The only reason you might not have the wealth you want, for example, is because of the unconscious decision you made about money when you were a kid. Remember this statement you completed in chapter 6: "when I was growing up money was…" Ninety percent of the time whatever you said is what your money looks like in your life right now. What money was like for your parents is what money is like for you because you adopted their limiting beliefs about money. Unconsciously adopted beliefs and decisions have shaped your life up until now, so why wouldn't you give yourself permission to consciously decide who you are, how life works, and what it's going to be like for you going forward? You might be doubting if it's really *that* simple. With 100 percent confidence, I can tell you that it is. You can simply make a new decision.

What Decision Should I Make?

The next logical question is, *What decision should I make?* Well, if your beliefs dictate your destiny and beliefs are decisions, shouldn't you just take some time to get clear on what you want your life to look like, in every important area, identify the limiting beliefs you have that aren't in alignment with creating those results, and make a decision that is just the opposite of the limiting beliefs? Shouldn't you decide that money is easy to make; that your body has the capacity to heal any temporary disease; that you will attract even more incredible people into your life; that you are loved, powerful, creative, and destined for greatness; that there's always enough time to do the things that are important to do; that you have all the resources you need to achieve the vision you have for your life? Wouldn't it be best to simply reverse engineer your beliefs and decisions starting with the end in mind?

In many ways, the limiting belief is a blessing. You know what you *don't* want so you must know what you *do* want. If money is hard to make, then decide that money is easy to make. If you feel like you're not good enough, then decide that you are good enough. If it feels like there's never enough time, then decide that there's always enough time. A powerful decision is always the opposite of the limiting belief. And when you make a new decision, that decision will change the way you feel, which will change the way you act, which will change the results you produce, and those results will always be in alignment and reinforce the new decision. You just have to be willing to give yourself permission to decide.

Don't I Need to Know the How?

The next question is, *But don't I need to know "the how"?*

Don't I need to know how I'm going to find the time? Don't I need to know how to grow my bank account or my business? Don't I need to know how to improve my health, or how to find the relationship, or how to get clarity on my purpose, or how to find good people I can trust, or how to have an easier life? Don't I need to know the how? The single most destructive assumption that human beings make regarding the ability to make decisions freely is the false belief that before making a decision you must know "the how."

In a study conducted at Harvard Medical School in 2009, researchers studied the brains of pianists as they practiced playing the piano and observed the specific parts of their brain that lit up. They then asked the pianists to simply imagine playing the piano and noted that the same parts of their brain lit up. This study along with others established that your brain does not know the difference between imagination and reality. Just as your brain built new neurosynaptic connections when you were a child to record the everyday experiences and memories of your life, so too does your brain build new neurosynaptic connections to record that which you imagine today as if it were actually happening now.

This is an extraordinary realization. The ability to memorialize your future vision through the act of imagination without needing to know the how is critical to discovering the mechanism or plan by which you will actually accomplish those desires. Put more simply, if you had already become wealthy, or healthy, or happy, or spiritual, if you had built an amazing company, lived your purpose, lived every day in peace and gratitude, published a bestselling book or created a nonprofit, wouldn't you know how you had achieved such a goal?

The single most destructive assumption that human beings make regarding the ability to make decisions freely is the false belief that before making a decision you must know "the how."

When you give yourself permission to decide without needing to know the how, you naturally begin to anticipate your desired outcome; you begin to imagine it. Conversely when you believe that you must discover the how first, you won't imagine the accomplished future until you first devise your plan. But by deciding and imagining without the prerequisite of how, your brain evolves into the brain of someone who has already accomplished their desires, and that brain change catalyzes the thoughts, ideas, perceptions, and synchronicities that become the bridge between where you are right now and the future you imagined. You create memories of the things that haven't happened yet. The decision comes first, and the how naturally follows.

The Power of a Changed Mind

When you identify a limiting belief and give yourself permission and are willing to make a new decision, you activate an extraordinary mental technology that I call the Power of Decision. The moment you make a new decision, which is effectively deciding upon a new belief, three extraordinary things happen.

First, your old thoughts and ideas begin to fade away and become replaced by new thoughts and ideas that are in alignment with the new decision. Decide you're capable of being healthy and you'll start to have ideas of what you can do to improve your health. Decide that things always work out for you and your unconscious mind will produce thoughts and ideas that are solution oriented, resulting in an easy and comfortable life. Decide that you don't need to do it all on your own and you'll have hunches and inspirations of who you could call to help you out. But continue to believe that you're not good enough or that nobody values what you have to say or that you have to work really hard if you want to be successful...well, you'll tap into thoughts and ideas that will prove those beliefs to be true. New decisions direct your focus toward the achievement of those decisions.

Think of your brain as a radio and your beliefs, or decisions, as the dial. Just as changing the station tunes your radio to a new channel, so too does making a new decision tune you into a new channel of consciousness that affords you access to new thoughts, ideas, hunches, inspiration, and information. If you believe it's not going to work out, then that's the channel you're tuned to and your thoughts will be aligned with making that hypothesis true. This is why life can become so frustrating at times. We have a new idea or intuition that we think will change our circumstances and it doesn't, simply because it's coming from a channel that is tuned to the limiting belief. Make a new decision, and you change the channel.

> "The man who thinks he can and the man who thinks he can't are both right."
>
> —Henry Ford

The second profoundly transformative aspect of making a new decision is that it radically alters your *perception* of reality. You notice what you believe and you ignore everything that doesn't align with your belief systems. Make a new decision and all of a sudden you begin to experience the same life you have, but differently. Neuroscience tells us that in any moment we are filtering out approximately 90 percent of the information or experience around us and paying attention to a small sliver of only 10 percent. That 10 percent we pay attention to is the information that is in alignment with what we believe. In other words, much of the change you're looking to create and the resources you're wanting to attract are actually either right in front of or in close proximity to you, but you simply can't see or access them because they aren't congruent with what you believe.

This filtering is a result of a part of the brain called the reticular activating system, or RAS. If you've ever bought yourself a new car, you've probably experienced the phenomenon of noticing your car everywhere. That's because this part of your brain is prioritizing your attention toward the noticing of your new car. This isn't necessarily a problem. But if your attention is prioritized toward noticing how things never work out for you, or how you're not a very disciplined person, or that the government is always taking advantage of people, then that's what you'll notice. And what you notice is synonymous with your experience. And what you experience becomes your life.

When we coach our clients who have been seeking relationships unsuccessfully for years, one of the first things we do is help them identify the limiting beliefs they have about relationships, or the availability of partners, or what they must be, do, or have in order to find a partner, or any limiting beliefs about themselves in the context of relationships, and to transform those limiting beliefs into new empowering decisions. As if by miracle, within incredibly short periods of time they find themselves meeting people who are closely aligned to their perfect partner by doing nothing else other than making a new decision. The old belief that "there are no good ones out there" or "nobody will want me" was creating such significant blind spots for them that their perfect partner could have shown up on their doorstep and they would have failed to hear the bell ring.

The same is true for our business clients who, upon making new decisions that "business is easy" or "what I have to offer is valuable" or "there are many people out there who need my help" nearly immediately find themselves attracting and enrolling new clients, most often from contacts they already had. In other words, the new clients were always there but were for all practical purposes imperceivable as a result of the individual's limiting beliefs.

The third incredible aspect of the Power of Decision is the ability for a new decision to create dramatic new coincidences and synchronicities in alignment with the decision itself. This occurs on two different levels: practical and metaphysical. By practical I'm referring to the fact that you have close to six thousand thoughts a day, most of which you don't notice. These unconscious thoughts play a critical role in your day-to-day, month-to-month, and year-to-year decisions and, added up together, the entirety of the experience of your life. Seemingly minuscule daily decisions—like which chair you grab at a conference, what time you decide to leave your house, how long you choose to have a phone conversation, what route you drive, or when you notice the need to use the restroom—create the timing of your life. And the timing of your life determines, arguably, everything.

The millions of unconscious decisions you make on a daily basis form the scaffolding upon which the entire experience of your life occurs, and those small, seemingly innocuous but, in aggregate, destiny-driving choices are made behind the scenes of your conscious mind according to and in alignment with one thing and one thing only—what you believe. Luck isn't random. It is a highly architected, intelligently designed series of small decisions that produce a beneficial outcome. The difference between good fortune and bad fortune lies within the psychology of the individual. Where one has empowering beliefs one will experience a seemingly synchronistic fortune, and where one is hampered by limiting beliefs we find an insurmountable series of bad luck. On a practical level your unconscious mind is manufacturing subtle choices throughout your day that will consistently produce results in alignment with what you believe.

A Vibrational Reality

On a metaphysical level, your decisions are also creating synchronicities and coincidences. By metaphysical, I'm referring to the science of vibration and what is often simplistically described as the law of attraction. We live in a vibrational reality. All of reality is energy. While we experience life as solid, we also learned in high school physics that the material world consists of stuff or matter, that all matter consists of molecules, molecules consist of atoms, and atoms consist of a nucleus with a number of electrons orbiting around the nucleus. What we also know to be true is that the atom is 99.9999 percent space or nothing. This book you're reading or the device you're reading it on is mostly space. It's almost nothing. In fact as we peer even more deeply into the atomic and quantum model, we see that those parts of the atom that seem solid are solid sometimes, but not always. And yet here you are having a very physical, very real experience of reading this book.

That's because your incredible human bodysuit came with energy or vibrational interpretation devices known as "senses." Each of your senses translates this "no thing" energy into "some thing" that you can see, hear, feel, taste, and smell, thus producing a miraculous (and simulated) experience of a physical reality.

Brain scans show us that each time you have one of your six thousand thoughts per day, your brain is stimulating an electrical vibration of energy and each vibration is specific in unique frequency to that thought. In sum total, the thoughts you have inform what's referred to as your consciousness (or the sum total of what you think and feel at an energetic level). That energy, your consciousness, is connected to the collective consciousness or the thoughts and energies of all humanity and influences other people's unconscious minds.

Think of consciousness as a vast array of radio signals being broadcast and received from each individual brain on the planet. Your thoughts are picked up by others, who act unconsciously in alignment with those thoughts. That's why when you think about someone they call or you run into them at the grocery store. It's why when you think about something good happening it usually does. It's also why when you focus on your worst fears they often become realized.

I will expand upon this later in this book as we move into an even more advanced understanding of how to reengineer your reality, but the simple fact is that each time you are willing to transform a limiting belief into a new decision, there is a change in the wiring of your brain and therefore the specific vibration of thought that you transmit. As you change your thought vibrations, all of life will begin to respond to that new decision to materialize that new decision into your reality.

The only reason you're stressed is because each day you continue to decide that you won't be able to get it all done or that bad things will happen. You're not pursuing your dreams because you're continuing to decide that it's going to be too risky to transition from the job you've been working for the last fifteen years to pursue your true passion and purpose in life. You're continuing to decide that you can't grow your business because you've practically killed yourself getting it to where it is now. You've decided that your relationship will never improve because, well, that's how it seems and up until now what you've experienced. Until you make a new decision you will continue to experience a reality that is absolutely congruent with the old one. Conversely, the moment you make a new decision you drop the only resistance that has been preventing you from creating the change or outcome you desire, *the limiting belief.* The key to creating transformation isn't to figure out how to solve your problem or achieve your goal. The key is to identify the resistance or limiting belief and remove it via the mechanism of a new decision.

All of your power is in a new decision.

To be clear, I'm not speaking about your decision to "*do*" something. Decisions to do are basically goals or intentions, and they have their place in creating an extraordinary life. But I'm talking about the decisions you've made (your beliefs) *about* how life is, how you are, how money is, what relationships are like, what it means to be a business owner, to work for someone, to be an only child, to be fifty, the decision that you're not a morning person and that there's not enough time. Your decisions *about* determine your decisions to *do*. You can make a decision to be a millionaire, but if you've also decided that money is hard to make, becoming a millionaire will become difficult if not impossible.

> **"The most important decision you make is whether you live in a friendly or hostile universe."**
> —Albert Einstein

So why do so many people consciously want one thing and instead experience another? To put it simply, most people are not aware of what they are thinking. On one hand, they want to find a partner. On the other, they believe there are no good ones left. Or they want to be rich. At the same time, they think it's never going to happen for them. They aren't aware of the unconscious decisions they've made that are incongruent with the life they want to create.

So how do you become conscious of something you're not aware of? The answer is simple.

Look at the results of your life.

Evaluate the results you are producing and rest assured that they are precisely in alignment with the unconscious decisions you've been making. What's more, if you look at any area of your life or any experience you're having and you notice your reaction to that experience, your reaction *is* the belief that created it. Your reaction to an experience you don't like isn't the effect, it's the cause. If your reaction to an experience is that you can't trust people, or that you're not good enough, or that you have to sacrifice your life in order to have success—those beliefs were there prior to the experience. The belief is the cause and your experience is the effect.

Oftentimes when our students learn the Power of Decision, they are hesitant to make new decisions. They say, "Yes, I understand this, but you don't understand what I've experienced in my life and how much evidence I have for my limiting belief." I do understand. I understand that the only reason you have so much evidence is because that's the way the human being operating system works. Once a belief is established, you will call forth evidence of that belief and become laser focused on that evidence. But when you become conscious of the limiting beliefs you've made that aren't congruent with what you want to consciously create in your life, then you can make a new decision. From that decision a whole stream of new evidence, experiences, and ideas will begin to spring forth and over time reestablish the new empowered decision as your new reality.

A decision is absolute. It's not a maybe. Like we saw in the definition earlier, the word "decide" literally means to *cut off* everything except the decision itself. And in order for us to do that, to cut off the old limiting belief program and replace it with a new decision, it must be done with conviction. How many times have you decided to do something that didn't stick? You were fully committed until life showed up in a way that reinforced the old limiting belief and you went back to "See, I knew it would never work out." You decided and then you undecided. The process of transformation is a faith-building one, and as such we need support to nurture the new, oftentimes vulnerable, empowered decision.

We need a framework for seeing that the limiting belief that has been holding us back was never true. We need a tool for identifying a new decision and initiating the process of rewiring our brain and activating new thoughts and perceptions and coincidences, and to be able to do so in a way that prevents the old limiting belief from supplanting the new decision. We need to rewire the brain and make sure the wiring sticks. For this, we turn to a very simple but powerful technology called the *Decision Matrix*.

9

The Decision Matrix

The Decision Matrix is a "mental technology" or tool. Technology by definition is "the application of scientific knowledge for practical purposes." Here we are using an understanding of the science of the mind to create change. Ordinarily we use the word "technology" to describe the latest app on our phone or fancy gadget. But the most powerful tech that exists resides within you and more specifically right between your ears. *You* are a technology, but unlike your cell phone or your wireless toys, *you* didn't come with a manual and so most of us go bumbling and stumbling through our own lives learning how to inefficiently use the machinery of the human mind from our parents. They were well meaning but for the most part totally ignorant of how your operating systems and features functioned. In this portion of the book I'm going to start sharing with you the incredible features you have available to begin to transform your life, starting with the Decision Matrix.

The Decision Matrix is a tool and a framework you can use to manage the thoughts, stories, and limiting beliefs that become activated on a daily basis and to use your awareness of your limiting beliefs to rewire your brain so you can permanently change your habit of thought. Remember, whenever you are having thoughts that don't feel good, that aren't aligned with the results you want to produce, you know without a doubt that you are entangled with a limiting belief. This awareness itself is the starting point because once you've identified your limiting beliefs, you can use the Decision Matrix to rapidly, radically, and permanently transform them into new empowered decisions, thoughts, and perceptions.

Imagine for example you grew up in a family where your parents always felt rushed, where there never seemed to be enough time. Your parents had built a habit of constantly feeling like they weren't going to get it all done. Feeling that kind of pressure on a consistent basis began to shape their personalities, and over time your parents became stressed and overwhelmed people. They then modeled that kind of behavior for you, and as a child with an extremely absorbent mind, you adopted their model of the world. You learned to believe what they believed by observing what they said, how they felt, and what they did. You became an overwhelmed person too.

So now, as an adult, you're working your job or running your business, perhaps you've got some hobbies or you have children that also require significant time, and of course there's the daily unexpected experiences of life that need your attention. A bill shows up in the mail that you didn't expect but needs to be paid, the roof has a leak, it's a family member or good friend's birthday and a card needs to be sent or a phone call needs to be made. Perhaps as a result of these things you feel on a fairly regular basis that there's just too much to do and not enough time to get it all done. Well, you're not alone.

Most people feel this way because most people have created a habit of experiencing life from a place of overwhelm. We've become so accustomed to the stress and overwhelm, in fact, that in many ways it has become normalized. Everyone has it, so it must be normal. But the things is, it's not. There's nothing normal about constantly feeling stressed, overwhelmed, worried, and not good enough. And the truth is that most people, despite the momentary joys and happiness they experience, are living in a constant state of *suffering*. And if we were to look at the thinking behind this feeling of overwhelm, it would sound something like, *There's too much to do. There's not enough time. I can't get it all done. And if I don't get it done it will fail, I will fail, and I will be a failure.* Sound familiar?

It's important to understand that the real problem in our lives isn't that we don't have enough time, that we have to get it all done, or that if we don't, we will fail. The real problem is simply this pattern of thinking. When we operate from overwhelm we are operating in extreme inefficiency and set ourselves up for the things that we fear most—running out of time, doing things poorly, and failing. In other words, it's not the many things that life asks of us on a daily basis that are the problem. It's *believing* you're not going to be able to get it all done and that you will therefore fail.

When you operate from overwhelm you by definition are operating from a low level of energy. You don't have access to your best thoughts and ideas. You cut yourself off from that quiet whisper of intuition and you miss the available opportunities that show up on a daily basis—those little synchronicities and coincidences—that are designed to help you navigate through the various challenges of your life. You waste the time you have in overwhelm instead of creative, productive action, and you therefore manifest the exact thing that you feared. The problem isn't the dynamic of your life. The problem is the limiting belief or beliefs that are producing your overwhelm.

What can we do to begin to transform these limiting beliefs—that there's too much to do, not enough time, that you aren't going to be able to get it all done and that you will therefore be a failure? The transformation comes from the simple but powerful three-step process of the Decision Matrix.

Step 1: Become aware of the limiting belief.

The first step toward change always begins with noticing how you feel. You notice that you've moved into some form of stress, overwhelm, jealousy, anger, worry, depression—a feeling that doesn't feel good. And then look to see what it is you're actually thinking. Remember going back to the Five Primary Drivers that your thoughts inform your emotions. If you've moved into any form of emotional discomfort, the only cause of that discomfort is a thought and more specifically, a limiting belief. You observe your inner dialogue (*What is it I'm thinking right now?*) and you notice what the inner critic or voice in your head is saying. What are you telling yourself?

If you're experiencing overwhelm, you'll likely find something like "there's not enough time to get it all done" or "I have to get it all done or bad things will happen" or "I have to get it all done and there's no one to help me." None of these thoughts feel good, nor are they in alignment with your desired outcome of being able to get things done with ease and flow and so you can identify these thoughts as limiting beliefs. So we can know that, while the thoughts may *seem* true, they aren't *necessarily* true. They are limiting beliefs. Step 1 is to notice that you've moved into some form of negative emotion and can identify what the limiting belief is.

Step 2: Make a new decision.

You must realize that this belief is simply a *decision* and that any evidence you have for the fact that it may be true is only because you unconsciously adopted the belief from someone (usually your parents) and that you have been accumulating evidence to support that belief while consistently ignoring any evidence to the opposite. With this understanding you can give yourself permission to make a new decision.

What new decision should you make? If the limiting belief isn't in alignment with what you want, then it just makes good sense that the new decision should be some form of the *opposite* of the limiting belief. If life is unfair, then life is fair. If things never work out for you, then things always work out for you. If you're afraid you might fail, then it's impossible to fail or you never fail. If you're worried about making the right or wrong decision, then there is no such thing as a right or wrong decision. So to continue the example, if "there's not enough time to get it all done," then "there's plenty of time to get it all done" would be a perfectly powerful and appropriate new decision.

Now you may be saying to yourself, *David, I just got through telling you that there's not enough time to get it all done. Now you want me to just decide that my situation is the opposite of what I know to be true?*

Yes. That's precisely what I want you to be willing to do, and your *willingness* is paramount to your ability to change your circumstances. You have to be willing to acknowledge that your current reality is based on your past beliefs, and in the midst of what you've created from your prior psychology you must be willing to make a new decision even if the evidence seems to be stacked against you. This is the turning point. Then, once you make a new decision, you're going to reinforce that decision using your own memories—the data and the experiences you've been filtering out—to reinforce the new decision. You're going to actually see for yourself that the limiting belief isn't and never has been true by establishing that the opposite of what you've been believing is actually *more* true. Once you're able to see that your limiting belief is untrue, there's no going back. This is the power of the Decision Matrix.

Step 3: Find the evidence that the new decision is true.

The third step in the process is to sit with the question, *What evidence do I have that the new decision is true?* By "sit with" I mean be willing to psychologically entertain the inquiry until answers come to mind. That's when the magic happens. Your brain is like a search engine, and if you inquire within for evidence to support your new decision, one by one you will begin to have thoughts and memories that become resurrected in response to the question. It may take a few moments to "tune" into the evidence for the new decision. After all, you're working against a psychological and emotional momentum that has been built over the course of your entire lifetime—a personal history where you had been, for years, experiencing one version of reality that "there's not enough time to get it all done."

Ask yourself: What evidence do I have that the new decision—there's plenty of time to get it all done—is true?

Well, there was the last time that I thought I wasn't going to get it done and at the last minute I was able to get it done.

Ask yourself again: What evidence do I have that the new decision—there's plenty of time to get it all done—is true?

There was that one time I thought I wouldn't be able to finish my project, and then someone else showed up to help and we finished it. It was kind of miraculous—I never even expected that person to help.

Ask yourself again: What evidence do I have that the new decision is true that there's plenty of time to get it all done?

There are times when I don't get everything done that I wanted to get done, but then I realize that I actually didn't need to get it done on that timeline. Things just sort of worked out where I had more time to get it done.

As you repeat the question and begin to source examples from your past where the new decision was true, you'll start to build momentum into seeing a different reality. You'll realize that you had enrolled yourself into this idea that was never even true in the first place and that any evidence you did have represented only a small number of incidences in your life that, when scrutinized closely, weren't really representative of the limiting belief in the first place. At some point, not too far into your willingness to ask the simple question *What evidence do I have for the fact [this new decision] is true?* and as you string together these reactivated memories and evidence, you will experience a new truth or a revelation—a new empowered perspective. It might look something like this:

I always have enough time to get the important things done. Sometimes I get things done on my own. Sometimes help shows up. Sometimes I learn that I thought I had to get something done on a particular timeline and the timeline changes. In fact, time seems flexible. I know that I have this fixed idea of time, but it seems like life works with me to accommodate the timing I have. I don't need to rush to get things done. All things can get done over time. Today

I'll do what I can do and I'll trust that I can leave the rest for tomorrow.

As you work the Decision Matrix, you'll notice that your energy shifts. You'll begin to move back into a resourceful state. You'll no longer be entangled with the fear that you won't be able to get it all done and that if you don't get it done you will become a failure. As you find evidence to support your new powerful decision, you'll notice that the new decision not only feels good (which means it's true) but is also in alignment with what you're wanting to create (for example ease and flow in getting your tasks done). As you continue to find evidence even more easily, you'll notice that the stress and overwhelm are gone, replaced by confidence and calm. Other new beliefs will begin to emerge. *Things always work out for me. Bad things rarely happen. I don't have to be perfect.* You are now in a powerful emotional state conducive to effectively tackling the challenge at hand. You have effectively used a Decision Matrix to transform your limiting belief and realign yourself with your new empowered truth.

Don't Rush the Decision

You must be both willing and patient with yourself and your brain as you access parts of your personal history that, up until now, your brain had little use for. Don't rush the Decision Matrix but rather be relaxed and curious as your brain searches for old dormant memories that support the new decision. The first few thoughts may seem small, meaningless, almost insignificant, but it is the beginning of opening the floodgates to a new perception and reality.

It is for this reason, the initial hesitation you may have to decide against the false evidence of your past, that I've taken you step by step through the nuances of your operating system. To help you build trust and faith and willingness that you do have a response-ability, an ability to respond to a limiting belief and transform it into a new empowered decision that will alter your future. That the only thing you need to do is make a new decision and when you do you will begin to find evidence to support that new decision as if it has always been true. To realize that your past wasn't absolutely real but rather just one interpretation of what was real.

Remember that part of the brain called the RAS? That part of your brain that filters out 90 percent of your sensory experience and only pays attention to the 10 percent of your experiences (and only those experiences that align with your beliefs)? That 90 percent of your experience, or memories, that you don't consciously remember contains the evidence for the new decision. Stored within the neural networks of your brain is evidence for the new decision, an alternate but forgotten reality, and you want to reactivate those memories and make them the predominant lens through which you view your new life. You want to stimulate the neural networks and create a new habit of thought or perception. In effect, you want to deactivate the memories and perceptions you've habituated yourself to and create new neural pathways that represent the new decision. This process is known as "neural pruning," and the Decision Matrix is the single most effective tool for doing just this—for rewiring your brain.

Like any new skill or practice, the Decision Matrix may feel a bit awkward at first. But if you are willing to try it on and to stick with it for just a short period of time, you will experience miraculous shifts and discoveries. Your new foundational understanding of how you operate, and your ability to change your future through the proper use of your mind, will be a light for you in those moments of darkness when the change has not yet taken place. Stay loyal to the reality of your inner power and capacity, and the change will be inevitable.

"The universe responds by becoming the thing you determined shall be. The framework of your preconceived notions is your only limitation. These are subject to change at a moment's notice when you have arrived at a new DECISION."
—William Walker Atkinson

Why is the Decision Matrix such an effective tool compared to other transformational technologies? Incantations, affirmations, positive thinking, meditation, reframing, and the many other self-help tools out there begin to embed new decisions and beliefs too early, before the limiting beliefs have been identified and removed. Have you ever identified a limiting belief and tried to brute force a new empowered belief into your system? Perhaps it was through incantations or affirmations, repeating to yourself over and over that *money is easy to make, money flows my way. I am wealthy, abundant, and rich in life!* What you likely experienced was a tension between the old belief and the new belief. Each time you try to affirm the new belief, the old belief pulls you back and the mental output and exertion becomes exhausting until you finally succumb to the old thought pattern. For many people this leads to frustration, hopelessness, wanting to give up, or thinking there's something wrong with them. Like planting a beautiful garden in a bed of weeds, the new plants soon become suffocated by the old terrain. In order to develop a healthy psychological landscape, you must do two things simultaneously: remove the old limiting beliefs and in that new space plant a new decision.

The Decision Matrix uses your emotions, which are oftentimes much easier to sense than your thoughts, to help you identify when you've activated a limiting belief and encourages you to simply "look" or "listen" to see what the thought is. It then gives you a simple law-based framework for transforming the limiting belief into a new powerful decision using your own personal experience as evidence for what you believe is true. Other practices temporarily shift your focus and attention into something that feels better but give no sustainable method for maintaining that shift. If you've ever gone to a motivational event and felt like your life was going to change forever, or a therapy session that helped you temporarily shift out of your stress or depression, or even watched a motivational and inspirational video that uplifted your spirits, you've likely experienced that the shift didn't last. You can psychologically distract yourself into better feeling thoughts and temporarily open yourself up to perceiving new possibilities, but you've exercised your limiting beliefs for so long that they've worn deep grooves into your brain. And like running water woven into stone, you quickly find that your thoughts and emotions return to those frequently run pathways.

The Decision Matrix takes you through a process of actually "seeing" that the limiting belief isn't true. This is an important point. Your brain is tapping into ideas, concepts, and perceptions that it believes will serve you well and ultimately support you in survival. It's looking for efficiency. Once you are able to "see" that the limiting belief isn't true, there's a radical shift in the circuitry of your brain. In a sense, once you see it, you can't *un*-see it. There's no faster form of transformation than seeing that a belief is untrue by overwhelming the mental landscape with evidence for the opposite. The new awareness established by the new decision and the evidence that supports it naturally align your habit of thought and perception with the new decision. As you no longer entertain the idea of the limiting belief, you create a space now occupied by new possibility where what's really true for you becomes accessible. Oftentimes the realizations you have in that new space will radically reorient you to yourself and your reality.

Sometimes you have to start small. When you look for evidence that money is easy to make as opposed to hard to make, you may need to acknowledge, even celebrate, finding a few extra coins in the couch or receiving a small rebate check you didn't expect. In other instances you may have to establish your new decision based on the fact that you can see that others have figured out how to make money easily and if they can do it so can you. You may need to realize that all people who first become wealthy were previously not wealthy. These tiny pieces of evidence if faithfully adopted will begin to turn the tide of your consciousness and beliefs and bear actual fruit in your forthcoming experiences. People mistakenly dismiss the small evidence, but it's the tiny examples that, when focused on and used as support for your new decision, become the foundation of even larger shifts.

You will know the shift is taking place when you notice a change in how you feel. As you activate memories and dormant neural networks that represent the evidence of your new decision, you will move from stress to ease, worry to confidence, fear to faith, and anger to compassion.

You will know that there is a shift from the limiting belief to a new empowered decision at both a physical and emotional level.

Below you will find a simple three-column outline of the Decision Matrix. Take a moment to try it out using one of the limiting beliefs you identified as part of your Inner Conflict or with any limiting belief you've become aware of while reading this book. Give it a chance and see what the results are for you. Don't worry—you can't get it wrong, and there's no way to do this perfectly. The only way you can mess it up is to not give it a try!

If you'd like to access an electronic version of the Decision Matrix along with some additional free trainings around how to apply it to transform your limiting beliefs, I've added some additional resources at www.DavidBayer.com/decision-matrix that you can download for free.

David Bayer

LIMITING BELIEF	NEW EMPOWERING DECISION	FIND THE EVIDENCE

The Decision Matrix

Breaking the Cycle

My business partner was threatening me, again. At the time, I was an expert in a niche field called domain development. I would partner with owners of high-valued website names that were sitting dormant on the internet and my team would not only build out a website but manage the entire business behind it. One partner who owned a particularly valuable domain name was becoming more and more unstable and aggressive, accusing me of falsifying our revenue numbers and threatening to file a lawsuit. I had invested so much time and energy into the project and felt like I had so much riding on the success of it that my days were filled with stress and anxiety. Despite doing everything in my power to try to placate the domain owner, he still treated me with contempt and disrespect. One day, I said to my wife, "I'm just so tired of being bullied." In just those few words, I realized there was no way for me to make the problem of the bully go away, because I had created it. In fact, I had been creating it my whole life.

When I was five years old, I was standing in my parents' driveway dressed in a cowboy hat and vest playing with one of those fake cap guns—a toy gun loaded with a roll of tiny poppers that would snap loudly anytime I fired. I was playing cowboy near the street and fired my pistol at a passing car. The car screeched to a halt, and two seventeen-year-old boys wearing black death metal shirts with long mangy hair got out. The driver pointed his black nail-polished index finger at me and said, "You do that again and we'll come back here and kill you!" Terrified, I ran back into the house crying to my parents. It was in that moment that the idea that I could be bullied was born.

When I was fifteen, the bullies would strike again. Two kids at my high school, Brian and Atticus, had it out for me, and each day in woodshop class they would find some way to terrorize me. Crawling beyond the purview of our teacher, Mr. Souza, the boys would sneak across the woodshop floor, pens in hand, until they reached where I was sitting. One at a time they would take swings at my skinny bare legs with their pens, plunging them into my defenseless shins. This experience justifiably reinforced my fear of bullies. Bullies were dangerous—*and* they could hurt you.

After graduating high school, I attended Columbia University and was recruited for the collegiate basketball team. If you've ever participated in competitive sports, you may have experienced a dynamic between players and coaches that felt antagonistic. Let's just say that the men's college basketball team isn't traditionally a place to look for authentic connection, compassion, and conscious relationships. More common is aggressive teasing, sarcasm, insensitivity, and, frankly, verbal and emotional abuse. And that's what I experienced. From the first day of joining the team I felt bullied, and I eventually quit the team.

As an adult, I encountered new kinds of "bullies." When I started my first business, we were having success with search engine optimization. But then the algorithm would update and our sites would decrease in the rankings, which would have a huge negative impact on our revenue. I remember commenting to one of my investors, "Google is a bully."

Everywhere I looked—from childhood to high school to college to adulthood—there were bullies. So it was no surprise that in my new partnership with the domain owner I was experiencing the same thing, except this time, having been in this work for a few years, I realized that if anything were to change it needed to change *inside* of me. I needed to transform this belief around bullies, and I believed that if I could resolve the fear of being bullied, or the threat that a bully would take everything away from me, then my outer world would reflect that change. The domain owner would stop bullying me, or he'd somehow go away. I didn't know *how* to accomplish this, but I was certain that this experience on the outside was being created from within.

This revelation, that I was responsible for the pattern of bullying that I was experiencing, came at about the time that I discovered the Power of Decision. Being a decent student of my own work, I knew that the next step in the situation with my business partner was to work through a Decision Matrix. I first wrote down my limiting beliefs.

If I don't make him happy, he's going to litigate against me. There's no way to make him happy. He has all the control, and there's nothing I can do. I might lose everything.

Anything that didn't feel good and that wasn't congruent with what I wanted—which was a thriving, easy to run, peaceful, and profitable business with a business partner that I loved working with—I wrote down. Regardless of how true the statement felt, I knew that if it didn't feel good and it wasn't aligned with the experience I wanted to have, then it must be a limiting belief. I then took each statement and made a new decision.

I can't be bullied. I have everything to gain. I don't need to make him happy. No matter what happens I'm going to be okay. I have all the control, and there are infinite possibilities in front of me.

I then sat for nearly an hour in inquiry around what evidence I had to support my new decisions. As a result of working the Decision Matrix, I had several revelations. The first was when I wrote down "I can't be bullied." At first it seemed to be the complete antithesis to what I was experiencing. But when I asked myself, *What evidence do I have for the fact that this is true?* I had a profound realization. In order to be bullied, *I* had to allow it. I had to be willing to continue to engage in the combative phone calls with my business partner. I had to be willing to read the verbal tirades in his emails. I had to be willing to entertain his attacks. In other words, it takes two to bully, and as soon as I was unwilling to participate in the dynamic, he had no capacity to bully me.

As I kept finding the evidence for my new decisions, it occurred to me how much I had actually benefited financially from this relationship. It became clear that if it was time for the relationship to end, I could trust that life would set me up with the next great opportunity, just as it had done in every instance of my life prior. As I began to have these realizations, I didn't have to find gratitude—it was right there in front of me. Without the fear of my limiting beliefs, it was easy to appreciate the domain owner and the possibilities that our relationship had created. After all, it was a result of my success with his domain that helped me to become further recognized as an expert in my field, which itself opened up new personal, professional, and financial opportunities.

As my emotional state shifted from fear to gratitude, I began having a slew of new thoughts, wondering if there was a way to "profitably" exit the relationship and eliminate this guy from my life while actually generating more income in the process. That would be something extraordinary. And as I kept working the Decision Matrix, finding evidence for my new decisions, I realized that all these challenges with the domain owner were culminating in a gift far greater than any monetary reward. I was finally confronting the pattern of bullying that had caused me so much pain and so much complication for nearly my entire life. What followed was remarkable.

I decided to stop answering his emails and responding to his phone calls. Within two weeks his harassment stopped completely. Within thirty days, one of my former employees reached out to me. He had saved up some investment money and was looking for a business opportunity and wondered if I'd be open to selling the license to the domain to him. My wife had previously suggested this as a possibility, but I close-mindedly responded that nobody would be interested in buying the license to a domain they didn't own, and it would be impossible to attract any other investors as a result of the domain owner's character and temperament. This employee, however, was the *one* employee I had who had developed a great rapport with the domain owner. Within ninety days of running through the Decision Matrix, I sold the license to the domain to my former employee, with the approval of the domain owner, and exited the relationship and the business, which I had grown tired of, while putting an additional $500,000 in my pocket.

Shifting Out of Suffering

When you shift out of suffering and into a more powerful state of being, you gain access to higher levels of thinking, feeling, and acting. You become a more vibrant person as you disentangle yourself from the limiting beliefs. You elevate to a higher form of energy and, as you do so, become a more powerful, intelligent, resourceful version of yourself.

The shift in my own life happened so quickly and so profoundly as a result of just one Decision Matrix that I spent some time looking back on the incident to see if I could framework out the psychological and emotional steps I had undertaken. I wanted to identify a system I could replicate for creating more miracles in my life and to see if I could teach these same methods to others.

It was in that analysis that I discovered five mental technologies (in addition to the Power of Decision) that together form a system for successful thinking and living. As I put them together into a framework for unlocking my full potential, I discovered that these were the same principles that the most extraordinary and powerful people in history had used to produce phenomenal results. I refer to this system as the Mind Hack Method—and it will change your life as quickly as it changed mine.

10

The Mind Hack Method

The truth is that most people simply don't think. They think they are thinking, but in actuality they are simply reacting habitually to the situations and circumstances of their lives. It is through primal, fear-based instinct that they are engaging with reality. They are blindly seeing their lives through the lens of their limiting beliefs.

To be able to think, however, is to have choice over the way you interpret or give meaning to your life—to be able to be thoughtful about your responses rather than blindly reactive. When you are reacting to your life, you have no ability to change it. When you respond, you develop the ability to transform your problems, situations, and circumstances.

There is a big difference between intentionally responding to your life and instinctively reacting. Reaction requires very little energy—it's automatic. Responding requires the application of effort and therefore energy. All change requires energy, and learning how to think in a way that produces energy rather than diminishes it is the key to creating change in any area of your life. When you are experiencing life through the lens of your limiting beliefs, it is emotionally and energetically draining. That's why it is so critical to begin your thought process with a new, aligned, intelligent, and empowered decision as opposed to an incongruent, unintelligent limiting belief. But that's just the beginning.

Successful people have learned how to think according to a series of thought processes that build energy. Unsuccessful people relinquish their ability to create change as a result of poor habits of thought. These people think according to what I call the Ordinary Model of Thinking. Successful people think according to the Mind Hack Method.

The Ordinary Model of Thinking

The Ordinary Model of Thinking represents the default mechanism by which the brain operates. It runs off what I would call the primal nervous system, meaning it is an instinctual, automatic way of perceiving the world that is predominately about avoiding threats. It is designed for survival but isn't conducive to creating an extraordinary life. And because it is the default or natural way of operating, it requires very little energy. The brain is designed to identify problems it perceives as a possible threat, and this tendency to prioritize threats is why as children we unconsciously created so many limited, fear-based meanings or beliefs from the experiences of our lives. And as we saw earlier, the starting point for this method of thinking begins with our limiting beliefs.

Limiting Beliefs

At the foundation of the Ordinary Method of Thinking are limiting beliefs. Things don't work out for us, other people can achieve or have but we can't, good things happen but don't last very long. So many of our beliefs originated from the scarcity, survival-based, and competitive environment of our earliest ancestors. Food was scarce, threats were ever present, and death was nearly always possible or eminent. As a result of our ancestral environment, our nervous system, perceptions, and beliefs were shaped to support survival. Noticing what others had that we lacked made sense. Worrying that at any moment we might be attacked by a natural predator or neighboring tribe was prudent.

But our nervous systems have not caught up with our advancements as a society, and so we still today carry many of our original programs even though they are no longer applicable to modern life. Most people begin each day having desires and goals but believing consciously or unconsciously that they aren't possible. They enter each day already defeated rather than excited, worried rather than confident, stressed rather than calm. They are already at a psychological, emotional, and energetic disadvantage before they even get started.

Problems

From the low energetic state created by limiting beliefs, the brain begins to focus exclusively on problems instead of solutions. Because survival is a primary and natural function of the system, very little energy is required to identify problems and threats. Solutions require energy. So if you are in a low energetic state as a result of a habit of a limiting belief and the draining fear-based emotions associated with it, the natural tendency will be to focus on and find problems, whether they are real or not. In other words, you will not only focus on problems but will perceive nonproblems as problems.

We've all experienced this at some point in our lives, and in some areas of your life you're probably experiencing this right now. When you believe that something isn't possible, you become dismayed, frustrated, and depressed and focus on problems. You may drift through your day or at best take some form of desperate or half-efforted unproductive action and at worst spend your time and energy focusing on and complaining about your problems. *Why me?* you might think. Well, because you've chosen to believe that what you want isn't possible and as a result of that bound energy, at the second level of the Ordinary Model of Thinking, you've developed a tendency to discover even more problems.

Confusion

As a result of the continual and inefficient expenditure of energy, you experience confusion. Clarity requires energy, and as a result of unconscious limiting decisions and a habitual focus on problems, there isn't enough energy in the system to achieve the clarity necessary to produce your desired outcomes or to create any kind of change. I'm not suggesting you operate according to the Ordinary Model of Thinking in *all* areas of your life. However, in any area of your life where you're experiencing primal emotions (feelings that don't feel good) or are not producing the results you want, this is the reason why. You can't see a way through because you don't have the energy or clarity required to solve the problem. Most people want more clarity around how to make more money, or to discover their purpose, or to find the right strategy to grow their business, but what they really *need* is more energy. Trying to solve the problem from a low energetic state rather than addressing the *cause* of the lower energy is the great mistake people make and why life becomes so frustrating. Any problem can be solved but only when ample energy is brought to the problem.

Questions

As the Ordinary Model of Thinking progresses from a dangerously ineffective trio of limiting beliefs, problems, and confusion, your system will move into increased problem-solving mode via the mechanism of survival-based questions. *Why is this happening? What am I doing wrong? Why is it working for them but not working for me?* Left to its own devices, your mind will begin to try to solve the problem by asking a series of highly ineffective and unproductive questions that in and of themselves simply perpetuate even more low-level and stressful emotions.

Questions are powerful, and the quality of question you ask will determine the quality of the answer. When you ask questions from a low energetic state, you will always get answers that perpetuate those negative emotions. We've all experienced how our minds, when left unattended, can become our worst enemy. The resulting stress, anxiety, and overwhelm compound and compel us into such a state of uselessness and reactivity that we either become hopelessly paralyzed or frantically inefficient.

Fear

Limiting beliefs, a focus on problems, confusion, and disempowering questions consistently produce the same, singular result: fear. I like to call fear "Forgetting Everything About Reality" because every time we experience fear, we can look back on the past and see that the fear was unfounded, and yet we engage in this self-inflicting process time and time again. Fear of failure, fear of financial insecurity, fear of making the wrong decision, and fear of rejection hijack the system. Fear manifests inwardly in the form of overwhelm, worry, panic, doubt, rejection, anger, jealousy, and a whole host of negative emotions. Fear—which represents the peak of low-level energy and lack of resourcefulness—is the point from which most people are taking action in the areas of their lives where they feel the most stuck and dissatisfied. And simply put, no transformation can occur from a fear-based state of being.

(Re)Actions

Fear produces (Re)Actions—frantic, unintentional, and unthoughtful behaviors that either entail a tremendous amount of "doing" that fails to produce desired results or similarly a kind of indecisive procrastination of inactivity. How many times have you tried to "think" your way out of your problems from a place of worry or anxiety? Very much like a tumbleweed, you likely drifted through these worry-filled areas of your life, aimless and unfocused, easily dislodged and without purpose or direction. Left unattended, this leads to depression, anxiety, a general hopelessness, or convincing yourself that your life is good most of the time—settling for something less than your true vision and desires and falling short of both your full potential and the abundance that is your birthright.

The Mind Hack Method

High achievers, peak performers, successful entrepreneurs, impactful spiritual leaders, amazing parents, kickass professionals, and phenomenal people of all walks of life operate according to a specific thought process. Despite the fact that we do it all the time, thinking is not well understood by most people. Successful thinking is a process that involves a series of steps, or types of thoughts, that when utilized properly achieve a desired outcome. Successful, happy people operate their minds in a way that empowers them to place their consistent thought and attention toward their desired outcomes.

The good news is that anyone can develop these new mental habits just as anyone can learn how to ride a bike, read a book, learn a new language, or develop any new skill. A superior mindset is simply a skill. It requires a system, consistent application, and practice. Some people are born with an unshakable mindset. Most, like myself, needed to learn how to develop it over time. Anyone can learn how to think according to the Mind Hack Method.

Mastering the Mind Hack Method is how you can affect change in any and all areas of your life. We'll now go deeper into each of the six principles to illustrate their power and how they stack together into a highly effective mental system for radically transforming your reality.

The Power of Decisions

As we discovered earlier in the book, all change and effective thinking begins with an empowered decision. Decision is the first and primary principle because it lays the foundation for maximizing one thing: energy. Your ability to bring energy to any situation in your life determines whether the current conditions change or remain the same. Where you've hit a plateau or where you feel stuck, you aren't bringing enough energy to transform the environment. A high energetic state leads to improved ideas, thoughts, creativity, inspiration, and motivated action and makes you and all your efforts more attractive to the people and the resources around you. Feeling stressed, worried, overwhelmed, angry, frustrated, resentful, and exhausted isn't attractive, neither physically nor metaphorically.

As long as you are entertaining your limiting beliefs, your energy or life force remains trapped and compressed inside the unconscious decisions you've made that are in opposition to what you really want to create, and you feel that compression as some form of emotional suffering. Resolving your Inner Conflicts by making a new decision unlocks that trapped energy, and that unlocked energy aligns you with new thoughts, ideas, inspiration, intuition, health, vibrancy, connection, abundance, perception, and synchronicities. You become more alive, more expansive, and more connected to life itself as you align your psychology and emotions with your desired outcomes and state of being. You become a supercharged version of you simply by activating the parts of your brain that are aligned with your desires and expansion instead of your limitations and fears.

Think about it for a moment. When you decide that you're doing the best you can, or that no matter what's going on in your life you know it's working out for you, or that no matter what type of situation you're in you decide that it's in the process of resolving—you feel better, don't you? You feel *more* energized. That energy enables you to think and feel and do things you wouldn't be able to do if you were feeling sad or depressed or angry. When you make a new decision, you direct your thoughts toward your desired outcomes and you create a fundamental advantage in everything you do. This advantage not only empowers you to create breakthroughs where you've been hitting walls, but it allows you to create in ways that are bigger, better, and faster than everyone else around you. People looking from the outside will wonder what it is you've discovered, what new supplement you are taking or new meditation practice you've found. You begin to expand into the fullest expression of yourself simply as a result of the unleashed energy created by the transformation of your limiting beliefs into new empowered decisions.

The Power of Gratitude

"Often people ask how I manage to be happy despite having no arms and no legs. The quick answer is that I have a CHOICE. I can be angry about not having limbs, or I can be thankful that I have a purpose. I chose gratitude."

—Nick Vujicic

Successful people both in business and life have trained their brains to focus not on problems, which is the natural tendency of the brain, but on gratitude—what they can appreciate regardless of the circumstance or situation. In our everyday experiences, the problem is never the problem. The problem is the meaning that we give the experience we are having. Successful people have developed a habit of attributing empowering meaning, or meaning that feels good and therefore generates energy, to the otherwise perceived problems in their lives. They literally *find the gratitude* and in doing so reshape their moment-by-moment experiences and position themselves in a state of high energy and mental activity, resourcefulness, and magnetism.

In each moment of your life, you have the ability to assign a meaning to the experiences you are having. The meaning in and of itself is absolutely arbitrary yet critically important in determining your future success or failure. Every player in the game of basketball experiences a shooting slump—a period of time where they develop a streak of missing shots. Great shooters give a different meaning to a missing streak than average shooters. The best shooters give every miss the meaning that the next made basket is even closer, for they believe that the streak must end at some point and that every missed shot is one shot closer to a make. Average shooters focus on the missed shot and attribute a meaning that there is still something wrong with them as a result of not having yet ended the streak and anticipate the next missed shot.

In the former example, the empowering meaning, that the streak is near an end, provides the player with the energy, focus, determination, and presence to more likely make the next shot. In the latter, the player is in a poor energetic state and more likely to perpetuate the slump. Both players are experiencing the same situation, but each is creating their own reality through the meaning they give to that experience. Neither meaning is more or less true than the other, yet the meaning that is given determines the likelihood of success or failure in the next instance.

In business and in our lives we experience the same types of slumps. Life is constantly bringing us experiences that, if we allow the brain to operate by its default mechanism, become problems. However, in every problem, there is a blessing, a gift, a lesson or teaching, or some other opportunity. The ability to find that gift is the ability to find gratitude. In choosing gratitude, you tap into an unlimited energetic credit line with the universe that fuels you with the vitality, energy, resourcefulness, creativity, and ideas necessary to create a breakthrough and find a solution to your perceived problems.

Remember, the brain is a goal-achieving machine. What you feed into the input the brain will miraculously achieve on the output. Gratitude is a mental method by which you signal to the brain that you want more of something. In brain scans, we can see that when people are grateful for something, the specific parts of the brain that represent the memory of that experience light up. The myelin sheaths of the neurosynaptic connections around that memory become thicker. The electrical impulse between those connections in your brain actually become stronger. The result is a conditioning of the brain to find *more* of that which you are *already* grateful for. As a result you activate more ideas in alignment with the experiences for which you have gratitude. You begin to perceive things in your reality that were always there that are similar to that which you are grateful for, and you begin to attract even more experiences, people, and resources in your life to appreciate. Finding gratitude produces experiences and results that produce more gratitude. The seeds you sow with gratitude reap the rewards in your reality.

When you experience challenges or problems, you have a response-ability to find the gratitude either in the experience or in your life in general, and when you do, you elevate your energy to a point that problems become nonissues. Successful people are able to take the energetic foundation created by empowering decisions to a whole new level by practicing an attitude of gratitude. Doing so gives them access to a very powerful tool, which is the next step of the Mind Hack Method.

The Power of Clarity

"The only thing worse than being blind is having sight but no vision."

—Helen Keller

By directing your focus away from energy-draining problems and toward energy-producing gratitude, you gain the ability to attain something necessary for change—clarity. You must become clear on what you want to accomplish, and you must eventually establish a path for closing the gap between where you are and where you want to be. One of the most common complaints I hear from people is that they feel stuck simply because they don't know how to change their circumstances and they don't know where to start. The solution to this problem is quite simple—to establish more clarity.

You cannot have clarity in the midst of fear, worry, overwhelm, or other low-level emotional states. Think about it for a moment. If you're stressed about your bills, angry at your partner, or worried about your business, are you operating with a clear mind? Of course not. And can you solve your challenge while being unclear? Clarity is an essential tool for transforming any situation. In fact, clarity is the beginning of taking the energies created by empowered decisions and a habit of gratitude and focusing it into the beginnings of change. Clarity precedes action, and action is the way by which we realize or manifest our ideas into the world. Want to start a new business? You must begin to get clear on what kind of business. Want to have a new relationship? You must gain clarity on what that relationship will look like.

When you engage in the mental habit of clarity, you are actually growing your brain. That's right. As you gain clarity from a high energetic state, you will naturally begin to imagine your desired future—speaking on stage in front of five hundred people, raising $250,000 in investment, landing ten new high-paying clients by the end of the year, gaining twenty pounds and feeling vibrant and strong, enjoying your favorite glass of wine in Italy while dining on the Amalfi Coast. As noted before, the brain records what you imagine as if it has already happened, and you begin to create memories or new neurosynaptic clusters that facilitate new thoughts, new ideas, and new perceptions that contribute to the realization of that image into the world. In many ways the act of gaining clarity *is* imagination.

"First comes thought; then organization
of that thought into ideas and plans; then
transformation of those plans into reality
The beginning, as you will observe, is in
your imagination."

—Napoleon Hill

Let's look at how to apply these first three steps of the Mind Hack Method using a common example. Let's imagine you've been wanting to leave your job, which is a good job that you've been working for the last fifteen years, to go and pursue your passion, your mission, and your purpose. Maybe you want to start your own consulting company or perhaps you're really passionate about building a certain type of software. You've got this story about how your job is safe and secure, but at some point in time, you make a new decision. You say, "I don't know how. I don't know when. But I know I'm going to transition from this job that I've been working to my mission, and my passion, and my purpose." Great first step.

From there you choose to live in a state of gratitude, which maximizes your energy and focuses your attention on the many things already working in your life. You have gratitude for the job you have, the people you work with, the opportunity your employer has given you over the last few years, and the skills you've developed even though you know that you ultimately want to create this new business. I like to say that the fastest way to get where you want to go is to have gratitude for where you are. By living in a state of gratitude, you elevate your energy and put yourself in a position to access greater levels of clarity around what this new business and transition might look like.

Without necessarily doing much, pieces of the vision will begin to unfold for you. It might be what this new business would look like. Perhaps you'd get clear on whether you'd be working from home or going into an office. You might have a vision that you'd be working for yourself, or perhaps with a team. You may begin to imagine what your finances would look like one year, two years, three years into creating this new business. Because you've aligned your thinking with your desired outcome and you've been practicing thoughts that elevate your energy, more and more would begin to become clear for you. This clarity begins to preprogram your brain and motivate new ideas, thoughts, and action. You are beginning to become the new person capable of creating this new job not because you necessarily did anything extraordinary but simply because you've gotten out of the way of your own resistance and allowed the natural process of intelligent thinking to guide you in creating change. And now things really start to get exciting.

The Power of Questions

> "Ask, and it shall be given you; seek, and ye shall find; knock, and it shall be opened unto you."
> —Matthew 7:7 (KJV)

Your brain is like a search engine. When you ask yourself questions like, *What's the best thing that happened to me today, who could I call to get support,* or *what's the thing I like most about myself,* you'll get an answer. The quality of the question you ask will determine what type of answer is returned. The question is the search query; the idea, insight, or thought you have is the search result. Search engines carry information in their index or databases of pages, videos, or images depending on the type of search engine you are using. Put a query into a search engine and it will search its entire database to provide an appropriate result. When you ask yourself a question, your brain will search against the database of your conscious and unconscious memories that, as we stated before, is stored within the neural networks of your brain. In addition, because your individual consciousness is connected to the collective consciousness of humanity and (as we will dive deeper into here shortly) the whole of intelligence itself, when you ask a question you have the ability to gain insights, hunches, and information that are beyond your personal experience.

Questions are a powerful mental technology. Yet most of us afford little intention to the questions we ask ourselves on a moment-by-moment basis. The mind is constantly firing off unconscious questions that we experience in the form of an inner voice, or the voice in your head. *Why doesn't it ever work out for me? Why do they have it and I don't? Am I making the wrong decision? What if it doesn't work out?*

These are common scarcity-based and low energetic questions derived from the survival-based nature of the mind. Like a loyal dog, your brain will fetch an answer to these questions from your personal history. Why doesn't it ever work out for you? The brain will bring to mind all the reasons it never works out for you according to its recorded history of your life. *Because you never do it right. Because somehow you manage to always screw it up. Because you're not smart enough. Because others know how to do it better than you do.* Most people, in any area of their lives where they are stuck, are not asking quality questions. And so, the majority of people get caught in the energy-draining, stress-inducing, pressure-filled loop of unconscious questions and unsatisfying answers.

The world's most successful thinkers have learned how to retake control of their minds, and once they've established a strong mental foundation through empowered decisions, gratitude, and clarity, they use empowering questions to source constructive and productive ideas, thoughts, and answers. One of my CEO clients was in the process of making a major acquisition of a smaller supplier. In the short run, the acquisition was going to create a significant strain on the company's cash flow and resources. About a month prior to the expected close date, this CEO called me to discuss the incredible pressure he was undergoing and to get my opinion on whether he should move forward with the acquisition. "I've been feeling so overwhelmed over this whole thing," he shared. "I haven't slept in weeks, and I'm not feeling confident or clear anymore about this move. All I keep thinking to myself is, 'What if this is the wrong move?'"

A question like that can only produce unproductive answers that perpetuate low energy emotions. When I asked him what thoughts came to mind in response to that question, he shared an image he had of the financial statements showing massive losses, of a board meeting where the board was chastising him for the acquisition, of what it would look like to have to let people go and downsize as a result of the "wrong move." Not only did the question not serve his intended outcomes, but it was also putting him into a state of fear, overwhelm, and anxiety that was affecting his judgment, energy, clarity, and creativity. What's more, unconsciously he was driving his actions toward producing that outcome.

"What's a better question you could be asking yourself that might lead to more productive answers?" I asked. He thought for a moment and responded.

"What are three to five metrics we should be paying attention to in order to ensure this is a successful transaction for us?"

"That's a good question," I responded.

He thought for another moment and came up with a list of five areas that he and his team needed to focus on in order to make sure the transaction was going to go smoothly. It was clear, based on the questions he had been asking, why my client felt stuck and was moving into a low energy state—a symptom of the Ordinary Model of Thinking. By consciously designing questions that would lead to productive answers, he was able to develop an action plan that would lead to his feeling confident about the business decisions he was about to make. As a result of becoming acutely aware of his internal dialogue, he was able to craft an action plan that ultimately led to one of the most successful transactions in the company's history.

Too often, goal achievers move into the zone of action before doing the appropriate foundational work. Most people try to achieve their goals or change their outer world while their inner world is cluttered with disempowering decisions, a focus on problems, a lack of clarity, and questions that produce poor answers. An overemphasis on "the doing" vs. "the being"—or your focus, thoughts, and emotions—is the number one cause of professional and personal failure. An effective action plan can only be achieved in a high energy state with absolute clarity and strategic, intentional questions. The details of "how" are an effect or a result of consciously constructing questions that are in the greatest alignment with the outcome you are wanting to achieve. Low energy and poor questions produce what I call a "re-action" plan—lots of doing that doesn't produce the desired results—or worse yet, these unconscious questions hurl an individual into a low state of energy resulting in drifting, procrastination, and inaction. Questions are the key to tapping into a larger pool of intelligent resources that contain the images, thoughts, ideas, and answers—the HOW—that will ultimately lead you to a breakthrough in any area of your business and life.

Going back to our previous example, if you've never started a business before you likely don't know how. But you can discover how through properly asked questions. Who do I know that I can ask about how to start my new business? What books can I buy or videos can I watch to learn how to launch and market my business? What courses can I take in order to learn how to grow my business? On the surface these might seem like obvious and intelligent questions to ask if you wanted to leave your job to launch your own business. But quality questions like these can only be asked if you are operating from a high energetic state, and most people who are thinking about starting their own business are so caught up in the fear, doubt, uncertainty, limiting beliefs, and potential problems of pursuing their dreams that they don't ask empowered questions and so stay stuck doing work that is no longer meant for them to do. When you're operating according to the Mind Hack Method, powerful questions can set you up for taking action with the one thing that every successful person must have in order to achieve success.

The Power of Faith

Success requires mental preparation leading to intelligent action. Without the proper mental foundation, all action is inefficient. The final step in preparation prior to action is perhaps the most important. Taking action from a place of confidence, conviction, and commitment is essential in achieving any desired outcome. You must believe that what you are wanting to create, whether it's a change in your life or a goal you desire to achieve, is possible. More so that it is inevitable. Yet there are imaginary graveyards full of ideas, aspirations, and achievements unfulfilled as a result of doubts, fears, and uncertainties that compel the defeated individual into either inaction or unintelligent action. Perhaps the greatest mental boogeyman that prevents most people from resonating with the energy of expected accomplishment is the fear of failure.

Imagine how you would be showing up differently in your life if you could relieve yourself of your fear of failure. If you knew that with consistent application of proper thinking you were guaranteed to produce extraordinary results? We have become socialized to believe that despite our best efforts, regardless of our intentions, failure is possible. It is this fear of failure that prevents us from fully committing, and it is the lack of full commitment that is the real reason most people fail in the transformation of their life or the achievement of their objectives.

Let me repeat that. It is the fear of failure that causes most people to fail, not the size scope, or complexity of the dream itself. Taking action from a place of faith—or belief that no matter how things look in the process, life is working for you—is an essential habit of successful people. They may not know exactly how things are going to go, but they believe things are going to end up well. Fortunately, in order to operate from a place of unshakable faith, you do not need to find a way to become more faithful. Faith becomes available in ample supply the moment you realize that failure isn't a possibility. The most effective way to overcome the fear of failure is to learn to see that the concept of failure itself makes no sense. When failure isn't an option, faith, confidence, and unshakable courage become the natural state of being.

Why is the fear of failure unintelligent? Because there really is no such thing. When you take action from a place of right decision, right gratitude, right clarity, and right questions and it doesn't go the way you expect it to, that's when something truly miraculous is unfolding. Unfortunately, we've been taught to call it failure. But really, it's one of four types of blessings.

The Four Blessings of Failure

The first blessing of "failure" is Learning. Your "failure" is simply a result of the fact that the intelligence that coordinates life knows precisely what you need to learn in order for you to accomplish your longer-term vision. We always learn through our experiences, but far too often we call this learning "failure." Yet we can look back at any point in our lives and see that all those things we called failures turned out instead to be important pieces of the process that helped us to accomplish, create, or become the most cherished aspects of our lives. Your failures were the pathway to your triumphs. (And some of them may still be in process!) A really great question to ask yourself when things don't go the way that you expect is: *What am I learning here that I'll be able to take with me to empower me to create the outcome I desire?*

The second blessing of "failure" is Redirection. You're being re-directed from one relationship to another relationship, from one job to another job, from one geographic place to another geographic place, and you're being redirected in a positive way. Again, I don't need to convince you of this. You can find evidence in your own life that this has always happened to you time and time again. There is an invisible guiding intelligence that is escorting you toward your vision that uses what is commonly misunderstood as "failure" to shepherd you to greater opportunities and results. Things always get better. But in the moment when we don't have that perspective, we think that what we're experiencing is failure and oftentimes miss the opportunity. It's simply a redirection.

The third blessing of "failure" is Reflection. If your beliefs and decisions are creating your external reality and if thoughts are truly things that interact with consciousness everywhere to manufacture the circumstances and synchronicities of your life, then sometimes what you're experiencing as failure is simply the realization of something you weren't aware you were thinking. In other words, if you've been believing and putting your mental attention toward certain things you don't actually want, then the "failure" that has shown up is affording you deeper insights into your inner framework so you can make the proper psychological and emotional adjustments. In fact, these reflections—outcomes we don't like—are a tremendous opportunity. It is in these moments that you can observe your own reaction to the experience, which brings an awareness of what you actually think or believe. These are moments of great self-realization and when treated as such, along with having access to the tools of transformation, you can make a different decision about life and catalyze a dramatically different and vastly more aligned future.

Say for example you were in a particular business relationship or personal relationship and things didn't work out the way you expected. When the relationship went south, you may have had a reaction like, *Things never work out for me. I can't trust people.* This is important for you to understand, because until you realize you've made this decision about people and business, you're going to continue to manufacture the same results in your life. This experience you're having, which you're calling failure because it's not going the way you expect, is the blessing of revelation. If you are present to it, you can realize that you've been making these decisions (for a long time) unconsciously. Make a new decision and you change your future.

The fourth blessing of "failure" is the Setup. This is one of my favorites. We are always being set up. We're constantly being set up by ourselves. This is where I get a little bit on my *woo-woo* (and I promise to ground this in a solid philosophy and framework later), but the higher intelligent part of ourselves that does not come into the physical body is constantly guiding us. That part of you which you could call your authentic self or your higher self, or intelligence, universe, or God, sits outside our present time-space reality and knows before you do what you really want both now and in the future. Because it has this future-oriented vision, it's consistently setting up the plan for you to accomplish your ultimate goals, your ultimate vision, your ultimate dreams. Oftentimes, you run into the setup and, because it's usually something quite significant and longer term, you can't possibly see how this is working for you in your life until you reflect back on it from some point in the future.

"People don't realize you are born to fail and born to get up. It is the goal of every spiritual being to try to live as big a life as possible; to love as much as possible; to give as much as possible, and fail as often as possible."

—Gary Keller

For nearly five years, I struggled with a health challenge for which I could find no blessing or benefit. Now, I see it was one of the greatest experiences of my life. It helped me form some of the most cherished aspects of who I am today. It's given me a much deeper understanding of how to support my students and clients who are experiencing something similar. Thanks to that "failure," I've created some incredibly powerful and supportive teachings and trainings that have helped thousands of people redevelop a relationship with their bodies and illnesses, ultimately helping them experience powerful healing and transformation. My health challenge has been responsible for generating millions of dollars, brought my wife and me closer in our relationship, and has helped me to become a better father. So the fourth blessing is the setup—recognizing that in all our challenges, failures, and letdowns, there is a guiding intelligence that is using our failures as fodder for our greatest triumphs.

The Power of Actions

When you get to a point where you truly realize and understand that life is ALWAYS working for you (and you will by the end of this book), you can take inspired action without the fear of what might go wrong because in reality, there is no such thing. Nothing can ever go wrong. There is no such thing as failure. There's never a right or wrong decision. The reality is that the only wrong decision is indecision, procrastination, or fear. When you embrace life and take action based on empowered new decisions, the clarity that you have, and the empowering questions you can ask, while living in a state of gratitude and faith, nothing can prevent you from creating a breakthrough in any area of your business or your life.

Action is a necessary and important part of the creative process. It is the culmination of all the prior steps in the Mind Hack Method. Through action we take ideas and we bring them into our manifested reality. Action is the ultimate illustration of our ideas, and through it we make the ultimate energetic deposit toward our desired outcomes. By taking action we make our next move on the chessboard of life, and we give life an opportunity to respond. This back and forth between the action we take and the response of life is what allows us to create results in partnership with life itself. When we refuse to take action, as a result of low energetic influencers like limiting beliefs, a focus on problems, doubt, fear, or procrastination, we eliminate our role in the creative process and deny ourselves access to the resources around us.

We must take action. Specifically, we must take powerful, joyful, faithful action that is aligned with the outcomes we desire. Far too often, the action we take is from a reactive fear-based place that can only create undesirable results. But when we take action from a powerful state as a result of the consistent application of the Mind Hack Method, our actions produce productive results, no matter what those results end up being.

Putting It All Together

When you consciously create decisions that are congruent with who you want to be and what you want to accomplish in the world, you construct a strong foundation to break out of the Ordinary Model of Thinking. By creating an alignment between your inner and outer worlds, you unlock a tremendous amount of internal energy. Because you have learned how to align your thoughts and emotions, you are capable of directing the mind's attention away from problems and toward opportunities and those things that are already working. You have developed an attitude of gratitude. Despite your external circumstances, you have enrolled the brain in finding the gift, blessing, and opportunity in every experience.

You see what others cannot see because you have created enough energetic momentum to direct the brain rather than be directed by it.

With this incredible energetic storehouse, you are able to achieve extraordinary clarity. You've identified what you want to achieve, who you want to be, what you want your life to look like, and why these things are important to you. You know where you're going and begin to understand how you'll get there. With this clarity, you take advantage of the brain's extraordinary capacity to source answers via the technology of questions. By consciously directing the brain through asking key strategic and empowering questions, you're able to source the thoughts, ideas, images, creativity, and inspiration necessary for your journey. The plan becomes clear through the use of proper questions.

With right answers and a clear plan, you move forward with an unparalleled faith. Sure of where you're going and how you're going to get there (or unsure but trusting in a positive outcome), you unlock the ability to take powerful and tactical action to produce impressive results. Oftentimes, you'll achieve so much in such a short period that you'll seem to defy time. But you are not defying time; you are simply leveraging the power of intelligent action to bring massive resources into this area of your life and create superhuman breakthroughs and outcomes. You choose the experience of your reality rather than allowing your experiences to dictate how you think and feel. You are the cause of your environment rather than a reaction to it. You have learned how to hack your mind.

If you're interested in learning more about the Mind Hack Method and want to go even deeper, visit www.DavidBayer.com/MindHack for additional downloads and free trainings on the methodology.

11

The Revelation

For several years we were using the Mind Hack Method to facilitate radical transformation for our clients and students. They would come in with a thing that they wanted (their One Thing), identify the resistance or thinking that was causing them suffering and preventing them from creating whatever it was that they wanted (their Inner Conflict), use the Power of Decision and the Decision Matrix to create new empowered decisions (thereby eradicating their old limiting beliefs), and leverage the Mind Hack Method to align their thinking and feeling with higher states of emotion in order to generate the resourcefulness needed to create powerfully.

The breakthroughs were often hard to believe: massive permanent shifts in people's businesses, relationships, health, and bank accounts in a shockingly short period of time. Decades of depressions and feelings of suicide gone within a matter of weeks or months. People who had been searching for their purpose for years discovering it within a matter of weeks. Our clients and students were experiencing a total transformation of their emotional and psychological experience of life, and as a result they were becoming more passionate, patient, intelligent, active, vibrant, loving, abundant, and creative people.

But not just that. They were becoming what any reasonable person might observe to be superhuman, operating on the leading edge of their companies, their communities, their families. They were attaining the ability to be unshakable amidst the chaos of any situation, completely undeterred by their external circumstances and unstoppable in each of their own individual paths toward achieving their full potential. There seemed to be no limitation to what was possible with the consistent application of the methodology, and as our business and reach grew we developed a certification program, teaching other leaders, coaches, and impact-driven people how to facilitate change using our frameworks. As more and more people came to our live events and enrolled in our coaching programs, we built a full team of in-house coaches.

One of my goals has always been to make transformation as easy and rapid as possible. I became obsessed with finding a way to create even faster permanent breakthroughs. With this as my focus, and with thousands of clients going through our programs and working closely with my coaches, I noticed something remarkable that led me to one of the most profound discoveries in personal growth.

We had seen that no matter what our clients were struggling with or wanting to create, the only thing preventing them from achieving their desires was a limiting belief. But beyond that we saw a curious pattern. Regardless of what their limiting beliefs were, no matter how long they had held the belief or how much evidence they had to justify it, when they worked a Decision Matrix to completion, each and every client told us that they believed that the limiting belief was *never true*.

In other words, once they were able to find the evidence that supported the new decision, each and every one of them saw clearly that their Inner Conflict—that they weren't lovable, that things don't work out, that life is hard or unfair, that people are inconsiderate, that you have to work hard to produce results, that it takes money to make money, that they weren't worthy of love or success—whatever their limiting belief was, 100 percent of the time after working a Decision Matrix *they* told *us* that the limiting belief was no longer true for them.

This seemed impossible at first. How could this be? Surely there must be some instances where a limiting belief was true. Some instances when someone truly wasn't good enough or when there wasn't enough time to get it all done. There must be some occasions when someone might make the wrong decision or be alone for the rest of their lives. How could it be that no matter what limiting belief someone had, once they decided the opposite, each and every single person we worked with believed that the new decision was more true than the limiting belief? And that's when we discovered the Two States of Being, and the speed of transformation took an exponential leap.

The Two States of Being

Let's say you went to the gym and loaded up far more weight than you could handle (and if you're not a gym person, that's okay, just imagine). Someone assists you in your exercise—a spotter—giving you additional support so you can move the heavier-than-usual weight. If you then drop the weight, say by 50 percent, to a weight that is what you're more accustomed to moving, you'll find that even though this reduced weight was something that perhaps you could ordinarily only do ten to ten repetitions of, you'll often be able to do far more repetitions. The reason for this is that relative to the heavier weight, the reduced weight feels lighter. That's what we're about to do with everything you've learned thus far in this book. We're about to get bigger, better, faster, easier.

What we discovered after observing data from thousands of clients was that they were consistently in a low energetic state when they were entangled with or thinking their limiting beliefs. Once they made a new decision and worked the Decision Matrix and applied the Mind Hack Method, they would shift into a more energized and resourceful state. After shifting their beliefs and making a new decision, they would look back on the limiting belief and indicate that they could now see from their more energetic state that the limiting belief was and had never been true. They would tell us that 100 percent of the time the limiting belief was untrue. We saw the same pattern, over and over again, thousands of times. That's when we realized that there were only Two States of Being and that, depending on which state of being you were in, you were either in misalignment with the reality of what was really occurring in your life or in alignment with it. And *this* had a dramatic impact on everything.

In other words, how you felt would determine whether you were interpreting reality accurately or inaccurately. And when someone was in a low energetic state of being, they were consistently misinterpreting the reality of their situation. By "state of being," I'm referring to emotional states. If we could categorize every single emotion you might feel, they would fall into one of only two categories. There are only two states of being. Those are Powerful states and Primal states.

There are only two states of being— Powerful states and Primal states.

Powerful states of being are states of being that feel good—states like joy, compassion, curiosity, creativity, connection, happiness, inspiration, calm, and peace. There are also Primal states of being—states like anger, stress, overwhelm, frustration, jealousy, boredom, depression, and fear. All forms of suffering are Primal states of being. You are always in one state of being or the other (meaning in a Powerful state or a Primal state), and you are never in two states of being at the same time. Check in with yourself for a moment and notice how you feel right now, in this very moment. Can you name the emotion? If not, that's okay. Do you feel good, or do you feel bad? What state of being are you in right now—a Powerful state or a Primal state?

Powerful states, states that feel good, are active when your parasympathetic nervous system is active. Your parasympathetic nervous system is often referred to as "rest and digest" and is predominant when there are conditions conducive to relaxation, joy, or happiness. Primal states, states that don't feel good, are active when your sympathetic nervous system is active. Your sympathetic nervous system is what kicks in under "fight or flight" or freeze conditions. In a parasympathetic or Powerful state you are conserving and increasing your energy. In Primal or sympathetic states you are expending energy. As we saw in the Mind Hack Method, any change you are wanting to create in your life requires energy, which means that all change you are wanting to create will originate from a Powerful state.

All change occurs from a Powerful state of being.

The first two Noble Truths of Buddhism state that "life is full of suffering" and "the suffering is going to happen to you." You should have no judgment about whether you experience a Powerful or a Primal state. You're not a better person or a worse person if you spend more or less time in a Powerful or Primal state. However, what is important to acknowledge is that everything you want to create—more wealth, greater health, better relationships, more clarity, greater impact, higher levels of leadership, spiritual growth, an improved emotional experience of life, better parenting, increased friendships, great works of art, business success—comes from a Powerful state of being.

When you are in a Powerful state, you are operating with intelligence. You are perceiving the situations, opportunities, and challenges around you accurately. You are able to access information, inspiration, and intuition that provides a great advantage to your efforts. You are enjoyable to be around, almost magnetic. You seem to be in the flow of life, in alignment with timing and luck. Challenges still occur but pass quickly and easily. Opportunities, abundance, and coincidence are the normal course of the day.

When you are suffering, or in a Primal state, you disconnect from others and from yourself. You seem to disappear into a dark space of the mind that is guilty about the past and worried about the future. As if in a dark fog, you scramble through your day seeming to attract obstacle after obstacle. You simply do not have the energy or intelligence to operate efficiently. Life feels chaotic, and it is for you, as a result of not being able to fully plug into and connect with the flow of life.

If you were to ask me what one thing you should focus on in order to create a joyful, prosperous, purpose-driven life where you were living as the embodiment of your full potential, my answer would be simple: notice when you've moved into a Primal state and use the tools and resources you have available to you to move into a Powerful state as quickly as possible. In a Primal state, you are operating according to the Ordinary Model of Thinking, driven by primal fears and concerns as a result of a limiting belief–driven perspective of life. The primal regions of the brain like the amygdala and limbic system are active. You're in survival mode, operating like our more primitive human ancestors fighting for survival. When you are in a Powerful state, you gain access to the infinite inner and outer energies and resources of the supreme man and supreme woman. You literally become superhuman.

I want you to think about how much time you spend in a Primal state on an average daily basis. Knowing this number is a critical starting point for your progression. If you added up all the time you spent in stress, anxiety, overwhelm—comparing yourself to other people, indecision, worrying you're not going to do it right or you're not enough, judging other people, judging yourself, feeling depressed or hopeless or even bored—how much time do you spend on an average day in a Primal state? It could be five minutes when you wake up, another ten on your morning drive, something that triggers you for a few hours at work, the debate in your head about whether you go to the gym, or whether you should eat that sugary snack or have that extra cup of coffee, wondering when things are going to get better for you, or getting lost in your head after noticing someone else's fake social media life and comparing it to your own. It might be when you're sitting in a meeting, or watching Netflix, or even having a conversation with a colleague or friend.

When I first began this work, I was pretty much in a Primal state all the time. Not because I was a bad or stupid person but simply because my nervous system was hypervigilant and had been conditioned to being in a fight-or-flight sympathetic response even when there was nothing to be alarmed by. I was a functional sufferer, still active in my life but not efficient. Certainly not happy. There were joyful moments in my life, but they were the exception not the rule. I had gotten so used to being tense that I didn't even notice I was stressed almost all the time. And what I've found is that *most* people spend *most* of their days (and most of their lives) operating from a Primal state, which is why most people aren't living the life they dream of and are falling short of their goals and vision and instead struggling with so many challenges. So my question to you is, *On average, how many hours do you spend each day in a Primal state?* One? Three? Five? Eight? Every waking hour? Even when you sleep? Stop for a moment and get clear on your number.

I ask this question during every live event, keynote, or talk I give. Having surveyed tens of thousands of people just like you and me, the average answer I get is six hours a day. And that's just the amount of time people are aware of it. Over one-third of their waking lives they spend trapped in the thoughts, emotions, and archaic nervous system of the primal man. And truth be told, as people get into our programs they realize the number is actually quite higher. But at just 6 hours a day, that's 2,190 hours a year. That's the equivalent of 54 (or approximately an entire year of) 40-hour workweeks that they're spending each year operating from a place of inefficiency and pain. In other words, you have access to an entire second life if you can learn how to reduce the amount of time you spend in a Primal state and learn to spend more of it in a Powerful one.

Most people have two major complaints: not enough time and not enough money. Well, I think we've found where all that time and money is going! If you wanted to take up a new hobby, spend more time with your kids, get a promotion at work, write a book, start a side hustle, get into perfect health, or learn how to speak another language, don't you think you'd have enough time to accomplish just about anything you desire if you could learn how to operate from a Powerful state during those 2,190 hours you're spending in unintelligent suffering?

I don't know what your time is worth or what someone is willing to pay you for your time. But at just $50 an hour, that's $109,500 of lost income *every year* as a result of not operating from a Powerful state. That's why this conversation is the most valuable conversation in your life. And here's the amazing thing—you don't have to actually do anything to be in a Powerful state, because you naturally operate from it when you're not in a Primal state. That's right. All you need to do is to *not* be in a Primal state. The good news is, there's only one thing, and one thing only, that can keep you in a Primal state.

Suffering Is Separate from the Experience

Most people believe that stress, sadness, jealousy, anger, insecurity, feelings of hopelessness, and frustration come from outside themselves. *The way the government is responding is making me angry. The way I'm treated at work and the workload is what is frustrating me. The absence of an intimate partner is what is making me feel lonely. My health problem is what scares me. The lack of money in my bank account is what's making me feel financially insecure.* We've learned to look outside ourselves to justify the way we feel. We believe the experience outside is the reason for the feelings inside.

If you've been paying attention (and I know you have if you've made it this far), then you now know it's actually your beliefs that create the results in your life. What you came to believe at the early stages is responsible for the types of thoughts you have now as an adult, and those thoughts create emotions. So the feelings you're having aren't a result of the experience but a result of the meaning that you're giving the experience itself.

Sometimes I find it helpful to observe how the natural world works. We can learn a lot from what we observe in the laws of the natural world, because what we observe informs us of how life operates outside the influence that our thoughts and emotions have on our experiences. It's worth observing that the kind of suffering we experience on a day-to-day basis can't actually be found "out there." When we observe nature, we see an environment where there is little to no suffering. Sure there may be physical suffering such as the pain experienced by an animal that has suffered an injury or attack, but what we don't see is the kind of emotional suffering that plagues the human experience. We don't see squirrels worrying they're not going to find the next nut. We don't see elephants comparing themselves to each other. And when we do find forms of grieving, for example, it is always with higher-functioning mammals that are closest to humans in the way they think. All suffering is man-made. Humans in their unique ability to give meaning to the experiences of their lives are the only species that suffer on a consistent ongoing basis. In other words, humans have the unique ability to introduce suffering into their own experience through the mechanism of their own thinking.

All suffering is caused by one thing only: your own thinking.

It is a remarkable observation, then, that all suffering is caused by one thing and one thing only: your own thinking. It is good news that this is the case, because it implies that your personal suffering and all emotions you experience that you don't like are 100 percent within your own control. Nothing outside you can affect your serenity, peace, and power unless you allow it to. You have sovereign control over your inner world and therefore by extension an incredible capacity to influence and change your outer one. That may not yet be your experience, but with the awareness you are gaining in this book along with the tools to manage your inner conversations, you are at the threshold of a new freedom of thinking. You've developed psychological and emotional habits, and those habits, like any habit, need retraining. But just as it was important for you to give yourself permission to make a new decision whenever you identify an Inner Conflict or limiting belief, so too is it essential that you accept that all suffering is caused by your own thinking.

You've learned that thoughts produce emotions and that all undesired Primal states are caused simply by your thinking about the experience, not the experience itself. The meaning, or the belief, or the story you tell yourself about the experience is what determines whether you are operating from a Powerful or a Primal state; whether you move from joy, excitement, curiosity, and passion into stress, overwhelm, anxiety, and fear. Said another way, the experiences of your life are like a black-and-white coloring book—they have no color and emotion. The emotion occurs when you add color to the picture, and that color is created by your thinking or story about the experience.

Over the years I've heard so many "yeah buts." *Yeah but my wife shouldn't tell me how I have to fold the clothes a certain way when I'm just trying to help out. She's the cause of my frustration.* At first glance, there may seem to be some validity to this complaint until you realize that the experience of a wife telling her husband how to fold the clothes better isn't the cause of suffering. The cause of suffering is the meaning the man is giving the experience—*that he thinks his wife shouldn't be telling him that.*

Having less than $500 in the bank account isn't what's causing someone to move into stress or overwhelm and feelings of financial insecurity. It's their thinking about the experience of the $500 in the bank account and believing they won't have enough money left to survive. Having a mystery illness or physical pain is one thing, but believing the illness or pain is going to last forever and negatively impact your ability to enjoy your life for the rest of your life? That's what will induce suffering or a Primal state. You can lack the financial abundance you desire and not be in suffering. You can be in pain or be sick without the suffering. Or you can experience the challenges of your life while suffering, which, paradoxically, will prevent or slow the creation of financial abundance or healing. What we find in each of these cases is that the problem isn't the experience; the problem is the thinking *about* the experience.

Let's take two different people. Both have lost their jobs, have no money in their bank accounts, and are on the brink of losing their homes. The one who believes this is the end—that they've lost everything, that they made unfixable mistakes, that there's no way out, and that they are going to end up living on the street—will be operating from a low energetic Primal state simply as a result of the meaning they are giving the experience, not from the experience itself. This person will be unlikely to find the resources to change the momentum of their situation.

A second person having the same experience might think about it as a new start. They may realize they didn't love the job they had. They may believe that all successful people hit some sort of bottom and then rise to the occasion. They may have grown tired of making so little money and now are motivated to find a way to create financial abundance for themselves and their family so they will never again be in a situation where they cannot control their own lives. This person will be operating from a Powerful state simply as a result of what they believe about the situation and as such will find the resources to radically transform their experience. Neither are wrong. Both are right. But only one will create powerfully moving forward.

When you change the meaning you give an experience, you change your emotional reaction. And the key to creating a breakthrough or achieving your goals is to align your emotions with power and resource, intelligence and inspiration. Those all come from operating from a Powerful state. The problem or challenge you face isn't really the problem. The problem is that when you give a meaning to an experience that doesn't feel good and you move into a Primal state, you no longer have the resources to change it. Your limiting beliefs literally create circumstances and situations where they come alive in your reality because your brain is a goal-achieving machine.

12

The Cause of All Human Suffering

B efore I take this distinction one step further, I want to do a brief recap. It's important to continue to reinforce these concepts as we build from one to the next, as you learn the entire framework for changing your life, through a changed mind.

You're wanting to create more in some area of your life, yes? And the inability to create this change or to be, do, or have this thing—whether it is material, emotional, relational, spiritual, or psychological—is causing you some degree of suffering. When inquiring into why you don't yet have this thing, you've identified what we call an Inner Conflict or a limiting belief or story about not being, doing, having, or creating this thing. But creating this One Thing or achieving this change isn't about discovering what you need to do differently to achieve it.

The transformation you're wanting will result from identifying what it is you're thinking that's preventing this thing and eliminating the resistance. It's about identifying the psychological and emotional resistance, your Inner Conflict or limiting belief, that is preventing you from your breakthrough and transforming that belief. Because your brain is a goal-achieving machine, whatever you believe will become your result. You can radically transform your limiting beliefs by acknowledging that beliefs are simply decisions and by giving yourself permission to make a new decision.

The Decision Matrix is a tool for creating this rapid transformation, and a new decision is the foundation of an entirely new way of thinking that the most successful people use to turn problems into gratitude, to achieve massive clarity, to ask empowering questions, and to overcome fear and uncertainty. This is how successful people think—this is the Mind Hack Method.

What's more, there are only Two States of Being: Powerful states and Primal states. The key to creating change and an extraordinary life is to learn how to consistently operate from a Powerful state. That's where your energy is and your superpowers are. When you are in a Primal state, you're disconnected from your power and you know you are disconnected because you experience a symptom of this disconnection called *suffering*. Suffering, however, is separate from the experience, and the only cause of suffering is the meaning or belief that you're giving to the experience. In other words, what you believe about money, time, yourself, relationships, your business, and so forth, is the singular cause of your feelings of stress, anxiety, overwhelm, anger, or jealousy. Suffering is the problem—operating from a Powerful state is the solution.

The moment you change the meaning or belief and make a new decision, you'll naturally shift from a Primal state back into a Powerful state where you have the resources to move forward and create a breakthrough. You naturally align your thoughts, emotions, and perceptions, and, via the mechanism of collective consciousness, you manufacture powerful synchronicities and timing to realize your desired results. Life begins to work on your behalf to co-create what you desire.

Once understood, it's fairly simple and straightforward. No incantations. No chanting. No meditation. No jumping up and down for three days at a live event. No coffee with grass-fed butter or coconut oil. All those things can be useful support tools in your continued personal growth, but here we've homed in on a step-by-step scientific process for transformation. You understand how to identify and transform your limiting beliefs, and you know it is a process of pruning the old neural networks and memories of misunderstanding and reactivating the memories of right perceptions so you can experience a changed reality as a result of a changed mind.

Aligning Yourself with Intelligence Itself

When you think thoughts about a situation that are untrue, you move into a Primal state. When you realign your thinking with what is true, you move back into a Powerful state. When you think that "there's not enough time and I'll never get it all done," you move into suffering. When you change that belief to a new decision like "I have all the time I need to get the most important things done, and whatever can't get done today wasn't meant to get done today," you move into a Powerful state. When you think, "I'm not going to have enough and I'm going to run out of money," you move into a Primal state, or suffering, and yet when you make a new decision that "I've always had enough, I have enough, and I will always have enough," you move into a Powerful state.

Why is that? Why is it that each time we entertain a limiting belief we move into suffering, and each time we identify with an empowered decision we move into a resourceful state? How could it be that whatever we think becomes our reality but that a certain set of thoughts and beliefs are more true and therefore, when we think them, invoke a good feeling or Powerful state?

The answer lies within our connectivity to consciousness itself. Everything in existence is energy. Our thoughts are energy. Our bodies are comprised of energy. The entire physical world is a shimmering, fluctuating sea of subatomic particles that science tells us is mostly space. This ocean of energy that consists of you, your dog, this book, your breath, your thoughts, your body, your home, nature, your city, the planet, our solar system, galaxy, and the universe is all connected into a single field. The Hindus refer to this field as the *akasha* and describe it as being "the finest essence that the whole world is composed of, the unchanging reality amidst and beyond the world." Taoists refer to it as "nameless, formless, eternal, the divinity in man, having no beginning or end." In Buddhism it is referred to as "thine own consciousness, shining, void and inseparable from the great body of radiance, having no birth nor death." In the late 1800s, English scientists described it as "the luminiferous ether," a mechanism across which light and thoughts traveled. This is why you may have heard of the concept that when you have a thought it goes out across "the ether" and others can pick it up as a hunch or idea. Modern science has been looking for a mathematical equation that could connect the theories of Newtonian and Einsteinian physics—to make all the math line up and work properly. They describe this as "the unified field."

In new age mysticism and metaphysics, this underlying power of existence or reality is referred to as source energy. In traditional religion it's referred to as God, Jesus, or Allah. In my twelve-step fellowship we described it as a Higher Power. In the movie *Star Wars* it's referred to as "the Force," Obi-Wan Kenobi, a master of using this force, described it as "an energy field created by all living things. It surrounds us and penetrates us; it binds the galaxy together." At the convergence of science and psychology and spirituality, this unifying field or fabric of reality that represents the totality of all existence (including you) is referred to as Consciousness. What I have found useful in my own understanding and journey is to refer to this creative guiding hand of the universe as simply "Intelligence."

> **"I know this world is ruled by infinite intelligence. Everything that surrounds us, everything that exists, proves that there are infinite laws behind it. There can be no denying this fact. It is mathematical in its precision."**
> —Thomas Edison

Whatever you want to call it is unimportant. What is important is to acknowledge that this Infinite Intelligence that operates as the Hindus say "amidst and beyond" our reality is a unifying energetic framework or matrix connecting all material things and, most importantly, that it *operates according to consistent mathematical laws and principles* (which I will elaborate on shortly). Your reality and everything contained within it is connected to and a part of this one unifying Intelligence. I find it helpful to think of Intelligence as a superorganism, extending its energetic tentacles through all living things, giving life to all life, learning from all aspects of itself, and having infinite experiences as one powerful, connected creation. You and I are a part of and inseparable from this Intelligence, and the key to eliminating our personal suffering, creating a joyful emotional experience of life, achieving our goals, and having a powerful living experience is to align our thoughts, emotions, and actions with Intelligence itself. To think, feel, act, and live intelligently.

The successful person operates in alignment with intelligence.

This supreme Intelligence, which is all around you, expressing itself through you and connected to all creation, has another fundamental quality: it is all-loving. The Hindus describe the resonance of this Intelligence as "om." Mystics refer to it as the original vibration and a vibration of love. Jesus's message predominately focused on interpreting this Intelligence as a loving intelligence. And if it wasn't yet clear by the description, this Intelligence is infinitely intelligent. It is working moment by moment for your greatest good, your greatest growth, and your greatest prosperity. Moment by moment as you freely express your will and make the decisions and choices that direct your destiny, this sum total of life itself is responding to those decisions and setting you up for your own personal growth and victory.

This loving Intelligence is orchestrating all of life to consistently set you up for character growth, guiding you to the vision you have for your life through the circumstances, situations, and challenges of your life, and nurturing and cultivating you into the best version of yourself. What this means is that the experiences of your life have all been highly calculated, intelligently curated, and brilliantly coordinated and designed in order to support you and deliver you to what you want. Sometimes quickly, sometimes more slowly, but always forward.

The childhood traumas, the atrocities in the world, the relationships you've lost, the bad business deal, the sudden termination of your job, the experience you had of tough financial times, your partner walking out, the depressions and addictions—all of these have been a setup by a highly sophisticated, infinitely intelligent system that is lovingly moving you through a life specifically constructed to help you realize who you are, what you want, and the full achievement of your desires and potentials. Nothing has actually ever gone wrong in your life, nor have there ever been any problems. Difficult, yes. Painful, absolutely. Are there some things you may not wish on anyone else or wish to ever experience again? You bet. But every experience you've had personally, and that which you witness in the world, is designed to evolve your own personal consciousness and the collective consciousness of humanity into a more conscious, loving, intelligent, and united human family. Reality, or life, is always working for us.

Circling back to the original question: Why is it that each time we entertain a limiting belief we move into suffering, and each time we identify with an empowered decision we move into a resourceful state?

Your nervous system serves as a powerful emotional guidance system. Remember that each time you have a thought, your neural networks are activating an electrical current that is stimulating that thought or memory. That vibration is sent from the brain through the nervous system, and you experience that thought as an emotion. When your thoughts are in alignment with the vibration of Intelligence or reality, the energy from those thoughts is *resonant* and you experience good-feeling emotions— Powerful states. When you have thoughts that are misinterpretations of Intelligence or reality, the energy is *dissonant* or in conflict with reality and you experience that out-of-alignment energy as suffering—Primal states. Limiting beliefs are these misaligned thoughts or, said another way, unintelligent thinking.

You've been equipped with a powerful emotional guidance system that informs you of whether you are entangled with unintelligent thoughts or whether you are thinking in alignment with the loving laws of an intelligent reality. When you're connected to the truth, you feel that connection as a Powerful state and experience vibrant, intelligent, resourceful states of energy. When you're disconnected from what's really true as a result of a limiting belief, you experience that dissonance as suffering and cannot overcome your challenge or achieve your goals until you change your mind. Until you realign yourself with what's real. This is why each time we entertain a limiting belief we move into suffering, and each time we identify with an empowered decision we move into a resourceful state.

If you're thinking something that doesn't feel good, it's not true.

Autumn had been struggling in her relationship. She believed that she married the wrong man and now, fifteen years into her relationship, she was seeking my coaching on whether she should get divorced or simply resolve herself to the fact that she would be unfulfilled in her marriage. I asked her what the problem was and listened to her list out all the reasons why she was unhappy in her relationship and why she would never find happiness with her current husband. For ten minutes I listened to her limiting beliefs, trying to identify some of the stronger patterns that might be at the core of her challenge. One thing she kept repeating stuck out for me: "I married the wrong man." She must have repeated the phrase half a dozen times. I finally stopped her.

"You say you married the wrong man," I said.

"Yes, that's right," she replied emphatically.

"Let me ask you a question," I said. "When you think that thought, that you married the wrong man, does it move you into a Powerful or Primal state?"

"A Primal state," she replied. She had been a student of my work for some time, so it was fairly easy for her to answer.

"Then we know what?" I asked.

"That it's not true?" she responded. I could see Autumn was doubtful, but the methodology had held up so many times before in prior challenges that I could feel her willingness to be open to the fact that maybe, just maybe, what she was saying wasn't true.

"So if that's not true, then what must be true?" I asked.

"That I didn't marry the wrong man?" she responded.

I wanted to push her a little bit further toward the truth. What I've found to be consistently true is that the degree to which someone is suffering is representative of the degree of unintelligence or untruth in what they are currently believing, and Autumn had been in a whole hell of a lot of suffering around this marriage.

"How about something even more polarizing?" I suggested.

She glanced upward for a moment, searching for a thought that would begin to bridge her back to the loving reality of her relationship. She took a deep breath.

"That I married the perfect man," she said softly. She sat there for a moment in stunned silence, contemplating what she'd just said. Because she knew the framework, I knew that she was already asking herself a mind-changing and relationship-saving question: *What evidence do I have for the fact that this is true?*

Less than a minute had passed, and I'd said nothing else, when she broke down into tears.

"Oh my God. For fifteen years I've been saying the same thing over and over and over again. That I married the wrong man. But," her sobbing increased, "it was never true. I made it all up. I had this idea of who I was supposed to marry and because he proposed to me unexpectedly and I said yes I just invented this idea that I never should have said yes, but the truth is he's amazing."

Autumn continued to cry even harder, sobbing. That's when you know you've had a good breakthrough...

"All this time I've been so cruel to him," she cried, "and he's been the perfect man for me all along."

All suffering is a result of
unintelligent thinking.

All suffering is caused by one thing and one thing only: unintelligent thinking. Not *some* suffering, not some time in this area of my life but not here in this other area. *All* suffering is a result of unintelligent thinking. Anytime you move into a Primal state or suffering, it's simply because you've been thinking something that's not true. I'm not suggesting there aren't experiences that we don't prefer. What I am asserting is that the emotional discomfort we experience, which is really the only thing preventing us from a more enjoyable and powerful life, is caused by believing something that isn't actually true. Disconnecting from reality or Intelligence leads to dissonance and emotional pain. Reconnecting to the truth realigns us with ourselves, with life, and with our personal power. Our ability to identify when we've become entangled with the deep, painful, unproductive unreality of our unintelligent thinking and our ability to reconnect to the loving, intelligent, always-working-for-us perception of what's actually occurring in our lives is the arena in which all personal growth occurs. It is in the moment when we see our unintelligent thinking as unintelligent that we create true, sustainable, irrevocable, and permanent change in our brains and ourselves.

The One Moment of Transformation

"I really need your help on this, man. I just cannot get out of this suffering, and I don't think the methodology is working!"

I had been coaching Brian for about six months, and we had been making massive progress. At twenty-nine years old, he was a powerhouse of an entrepreneur having already built three $10 million+ businesses and now running the third largest and fastest-growing company in a multibillion-dollar industry. Brian grew up in the United States as an Arab Muslim and, as a result of his cultural and religious differences with most people, always felt like an outsider. We had made tremendous progress around his self-confidence, which was having dramatic positive impacts on his relationships with his employees, investors, family, and girlfriend.

"What do you mean the methodology doesn't work?" I asked.

"Well, I'm out at this private event. It's me and like a dozen other people. I mean these guys were heavy hitters—the number one real estate broker in Miami, the president of the professional sports team, the number one DJ in South Beach, the mayor—all number ones. And I'm sitting there at this private get-together and I have this thought like, *These people are so incredible, they're so impressive, why did they invite me here?* And then it starts."

"What starts?" I asked him.

"The thoughts," he said. "I start having all these thoughts around how I'm not as far along as I should be, comparing myself to these people, and then I catch myself. I'm like, 'Okay here we go. I know what's going on here,' and I noticed I moved into suffering. I moved into a Primal state."

Brian had learned to really work the methodology effectively and had been doing great work. "So then what happened?" I asked.

"I remember when I move into a Primal state, the only cause of it is my own thinking. So I go and I look at the thinking."

"Good so far," I said. "What were you thinking?"

"I'm sitting there thinking to myself, 'I don't belong here.' Like these people are all tier-one successful people at the top of their game and I don't belong here."

"So what happened next?" I asked.

"I remembered that you said the thinking that causes suffering is unintelligent thinking. It's not true. And that if it's not true, then the opposite of it must be true."

At this point I'm waiting for the breakthrough. Brian's got the framework down, he's using it, he's at the last step. He just has to make a new decision or identify what the opposite of the unintelligent thinking is.

"So what did you see? What did you come up with?" I asked.

"And that's the thing, man. Nothing. I came up with nothing. To me it was one hundred percent true. I didn't belong at this party. I just didn't belong there."

Because I had been working with Brian for a while, I could see where we needed to go. We needed to get to some sort of new decision that he *did* belong there. We had to see the unintelligence of his unintelligent thinking. But the power of the methodology isn't that I do that for him; it's that he sees it for himself. My job was to simply guide him there.

"You're a religious guy, right, Brian? You believe in God, don't you?"

"Absolutely," he said.

"And your God, is He an all-knowing, omnipotent, omniscient type of God?"

"Yeah, of course."

"So then how did your God, who is all knowing and all seeing, put you in a place that you didn't belong last night?"

There was a long pause on the other end of the phone. I could literally feel Brian's head spinning, trying to process what I said as things started rewiring. Then it hit him.

"I see it!" Brian said. "I see how unintelligent the thoughts were. The idea that I didn't belong at that party last night. Of course I belonged there; it just doesn't make any sense otherwise!"

"Why?" I asked. "What did you discover?"

"I saw the truth, brother. I saw the truth that *I belong everywhere I am.*"

Unconvincing the Untruths

There's something beautiful about not trying to convince yourself that something is true but instead unconvincing yourself of something that is untrue. I could never have seen what Brian saw for himself. I had assumed he would just come to the conclusion that he belonged at the party. Instead, when he saw the unintelligence of the belief that he didn't "belong" where he was, it dissolved. What was left in the space was truly a revelation, both for him, for me, and perhaps now for you. Something profound was revealed that had always been there, the ignorance of which had caused Brian a lifetime of pain.

Since he was a child, Brian never felt like he belonged. He was different than the kids around him. He was Muslim. He was Arab. He was brighter than most kids his age. He started his first business at fifteen years old. He was ferocious. He didn't relate well to others, and they had a hard time relating to him. And he gave a meaning to that difference that didn't serve him—that he didn't belong. And in a matter of ten minutes, a simple framework allowed him to see the untruth of his limiting belief. And once that was gone, something beautiful was discovered underneath the smoldering wreckage of his old thinking. A single, simple, profound gem—that Brian belonged *everywhere he was.*

There is only one moment of transformation. Regardless of what tool you use, what event you attend, what book you read, what therapy you apply, all transformation comes down to one moment: the moment you change your perception. It is the moment when you experience something you've been experiencing one way, usually for a long time, in a new way. It is the moment when you see your unintelligent thinking as unintelligent. It is the moment when the meaning that has shaped the way you view your world changes, and it happens in an instant.

Oftentimes we can change the way we view things, but only for a little while. This has historically been the challenge with Personal Development 1.0—we experience temporary change but revert back to the same old way of thinking, the same brain structure, after a short period of time. The change doesn't last. What we are all seeking is longer, more permanent and sustainable change. To become someone different and to think differently without having to convince ourselves of our new beliefs or new stories. And there is a way to create long-term sustainable and consistent change in the way you think, feel, and act. To permanently rewire the neural networks and transform the memories that have been shaping the way you view yourself and your life. That permanent, powerful method, which happens in an instant, is to see your unintelligent thinking as unintelligent. The moment you do, everything changes.

Your brain is wanting to operate as efficiently as possible. When shown that the way it is operating isn't effective for your own survival, or that the concepts it's operating off of are faulty or untrue, the conscious and unconscious mind will no longer pursue the same line of thinking. In other words, if you can, through the use of a framework, see for yourself that your limiting beliefs truly don't make logical sense, they will no longer be your go-to lens of perception. That's why seeing your own thinking as untrue is the mechanism by which you create the most permanent and sustainable psychological and emotional changes. Once you see your own thinking as unintelligent, you can't unsee it.

Both the Two States of Being and the Power of Decision, which are really two paths to the same outcome, help you to identify the untrue thinking that is the only cause of your suffering and the only thing preventing you from creating what you want. Through a series of simple, powerful steps and a few key distinctions, you're able to not just identify your thinking but you're able to work with the thinking in a way that allows you to view it differently than how you've viewed it before. If the thinking doesn't feel good, and it's not congruent with what you want, you observe the thinking through the lens of knowing that not only is it untrue, but the opposite, therefore, must be true.

Now that you understand how the human being operating system works, you give yourself permission to make a new decision, and you use the evidence of your actual life to find evidence for the fact that your new belief is true. Through the process, you're able to see that the limiting belief you once held as absolute is no longer true for you. This new right perception, aligned with intelligent thoughts and actions and the laws of Intelligence itself, creates alignment in your nervous system, which you experience as a Powerful state. Now, free from suffering and energized and in alignment with right action, you connect with the field of Intelligence and the necessary co-creating forces needed to create change in any circumstance: to achieve your goals, to heal your body, to attract or mend a relationship, to discover your purpose, to create financial abundance, to have a more peaceful experience of life, to attract an investor, to create a more loving relationship with your children, to overcome your grief.

You have the tools, skills, and the practice to consistently use the experiences around you to deepen your alignment with yourself and with Intelligence. You've become someone who resonates at a high vibrational level. Someone who operates with intelligent thought and action. Someone who is alive with ambition and love and curiosity. Someone who instinctively knows how to handle situations that may have baffled you before. Fear of relationships and financial insecurity leave you. You begin to create a masterpiece life that others, looking from the outside in, admire and yet can't quite understand. Things seem to go so well for you, and even when they do not, you seem to have a constitutional capacity to stand unshakable even in the midst of change and chaos. You have capacity that is increased beyond the norm, and there is something different about you.

People want to be around you, they want to be in your presence, because you've pruned the old, primal, low-vibrational parts of your nervous system and you've redesigned yourself into a powerful human being. You are no longer reacting to your circumstances but consciously responding to them. It seems based on observation that you are dictating the circumstances around you. You've completely transformed who you were, and you've reengineered your reality to accommodate the life and the dreams that you have for yourself, your family, and the world. You're consciously creating a life you love and that others love being a part of. You've become a Phenomenon.

13

Becoming a Phenomenon

On your path to becoming a Phenomenon, there are four stages of development. Each stage represents a new level of change in your nervous system. An expansion of your consciousness. I asked you earlier: How much time do you spend in a Primal state? As I mentioned before, the average answer across a survey of tens of thousands of live event attendees and coaching clients is approximately six hours a day. I myself prior to getting into this work would have answered that I was spending twenty-four hours a day in suffering, including when I was asleep!

I've been able to identify four stages of growth that correlate to the amount of time you spend in a Primal state. I preface this by saying that there should be no judgment around where you are in your journey. Progression from each stage can be rapid for the dedicated and disciplined student. What's important is to be rigorously honest with where you are in the progression and clear on what the next step in that progression is. Here are the four stages of consciousness:

Stage 1: ASLEEP

6 or more hours in a Primal state

Stage 1 is where most people come into this work, even when they've been doing the self-help thing for many years. You haven't yet developed the skills for higher-level, more acute self-awareness. In other words, to be aware of what you are thinking. And as such you are spending six or more hours a day in a Primal state. At least a third of your waking hours are wasted on unintelligent thoughts and limiting beliefs, and as a result there are usually major gaps in your life satisfaction and significant financial, relationship, or health challenges. You are spending far too much time in a sympathetic state, and that stress and low-vibrational activity is yielding undesired results.

Stage 2: AWARE

1 to 6 hours in a Primal state

At Stage 2 you are more acutely aware of your thinking on a moment-by-moment basis. You are using the Power of Decision, the Mind Hack Method, and the Two States of Being as tools to identify when you've become entangled with a limiting belief, to begin to make new decisions, and to find evidence for those new decisions. You are slowly pruning the old neural networks and replacing them with new and revised memories. As a result, your nervous system is engaged more often in parasympathetic and Powerful states of being. Things are beginning to shift not only in your internal emotional and psychological experience of life but also externally. Where you were addictively engaged in behaviors like comparing, self-sabotage, procrastination, insecurity, jealousy, and anger, you are now finding footholds and extended periods of time feeling self-confident, compassionate, understanding, and curious and taking more consistent and persistent action toward the achievement of your goals and dreams.

Life feels lighter, and as such your relationships invigorate. People enjoy being around you and, no longer ashamed, you enjoy being around others. It is at this stage that you may decide to make a career change, pursue new hobbies or passions, start your own business, or find a new relationship. Health problems improve, and challenges that once confronted you seem no longer complex. The improvements motivate even deeper commitment to using the frameworks and the methodology, and in that process, like our friend Brian, new profound discoveries and awareness are made. A consistent observation of "becoming more spiritual" occurs. There is a deeper sense of relationship with self, with others, and with a power greater than yourself. Feelings of loneliness and self-pity slip away as dramatic change begins to unfold, simply by shaving a few hours of suffering off of each day.

Stage 3: AWAKE

Less than 1 hour in a Primal state

At Stage 3 the old personality has nearly completely receded into the history of who you once were. You can see clearly that the experiences in your life of trauma, abuse, challenge, difficulty, and discomfort were all part of life's loving design put in place as crucial stepping stones necessary for your character development and to become the person capable of achieving your goals and dreams. With little to no daily effort, you feel deeply connected to life and are able to see that life is working for your greatest growth, prosperity, and evolution in your daily experiences. You march forward with your plans to create, to contribute, to become prosperous, and to express yourself creatively, knowing that plans are helpful but that ultimately there is a greater plan at work. You have developed a capacity to surrender each day to that greater plan.

You are co-creating with life itself and appreciating the incredible synchronicities that occur along the way, accepting the changes in direction and plan as they arise. You aren't devoid of challenges, but you handle them with grace. You intuitively know when you should take action and when you should surrender control. At this stage miracles occur: disease remission, recovered relationships, radical increases in financial abundance, new business and philanthropic ideas. In this stage you are living in flow with the flow of life itself. And as you continue to live in the practice of observing your emotions, identifying your resistance, and transforming your beliefs on a daily basis by taking inventory of your thoughts and emotions, your nervous system evolves to such a point that you are living in direct contact and communion with Intelligence or Higher Power itself. As you do this, you become the expression of your own personal genius, guided intuitively, with a resiliency to withstand external chaos and to command and become the environment rather than struggle to operate within it. You're living in your spiritual practice and have become the convergence of your own individual expression of intelligence (YOU) and Intelligence itself.

Stage 4: PHENOMENON

When you have trained your perception and nervous system to the extent that you are able to experience your life as a series of circumstances designed to move you toward your greatest growth, prosperity, and evolution, and when you therefore no longer expend your energy on unnecessary fight-or-flight-based reactions to life (and to your own thoughts, for that matter), that energy redirects itself into emergent properties and qualities that seem to be supernatural. The irony is that these qualities are not an aberration of what humans are capable of but an expression of the natural state of the supreme man or supreme woman. The anomaly is the average person who struggles through life in suffering. When you aren't spending your minutes, days, and weeks driven by a reactive sympathetic nervous system, you experience the manifestation of that untapped energy in a variety of forms.

As we outlined in the Mind Hack Method, you begin to naturally view life through the lens of opportunity instead of limitation, gratitude instead of complaining and problems. Without great effort you have access to deeper levels of clarity. Without the static disruption of your incessant worry and limiting beliefs, you're able to receive or tap into thoughts and ideas that are in alignment with the goals you want to achieve. Your intuition increases with hunches and insights you receive directly from the larger part of Intelligence that you are now more closely connected to, which exists outside your physical three-dimensional space and time reality. In other words, the part of you that has already experienced your future begins to guide you toward it. Your body is at rest rather than under duress, and your physiological systems become more efficient creating health, vibrancy, and vitality. Your thoughts and your nervous system are resonant with the vibration of what you want and as such, synchronicities, coincidences, and timing lean in your favor.

Your level of creativity dramatically increases. Your speech and actions are intelligent. You seem to have all the luck. And as a clear, healthy, vibrant, joyful, attractive, magnetic, intelligent person, you have developed the capacity to operate at what seems to be a level far superior to the average person. To the rest of the world you've become a Phenomenon. And in fact you have. You are no longer the person you were, but you are the person you were capable of becoming. Someone deeply connected to a power greater than yourself, a living embodiment of Intelligence itself. You have become the expression of your own personal genius or greatness not because you learned how to become superior but because you simply stopped doing the thinking that was creating the facade of inferiority. You have become one with the Phenomenon of life or Intelligence itself. You are now having what I call a powerful living experience.

Having a Powerful Living Experience

There are two steps to having a powerful living experience. The first is to identify and transform the limiting beliefs and perceptions that are creating your own personal suffering and preventing you from creating the life you desire so that you can fully unlock the inherent qualities within you that enable you to operate as a Phenomenon. The second step is to now emerge into the dynamic of life as a new being and to understand the mathematical principles that govern creation so that you can harness them to powerfully create whatever it is you desire. To truly understand the natural creative forces so that, as a powerful creator, you can work with them to perform extraordinary feats of greatness, become a driving force for good in the world, and achieve your full potential.

Once you understand and unlock you, the next step is to understand and align with the principles that structure reality itself. In the early 1900s Napoleon Hill in *Think and Grow Rich* talked about how the most powerful people in the world understood that their thoughts created their reality. A century later in the early 2000s, the idea of the law of attraction, or how what you think creates the circumstances of your life, became popularized by the book and then the movie *The Secret*. In part III of this book, I'm going to take these concepts and ground them in the latest scientific theories to show you how to engage with life at a new level so you are no longer reacting to it but creating, shaping, and sculpting it in the most powerful, profound, and world-changing ways.

If you'd like to know more about how to experience this transformation live over the course of three full days, you can visit www.powerful-livingexperience.com to learn more about our flagship transformational event.

PART III

Reengineering Your Reality

14

The Law of Attraction

By the time I hit my late twenties I was broke, having wasted most of the money I had earned from my earlier business successes on imprudent things. At that time I was living in Orlando, Florida, and had planned a trip with a few friends to go down for a party weekend in South Beach, Miami. Miami was, and still is, a place of showcased opulence. Expensive cars, insanely high-priced bottles of alcohol, the latest expensive fashions, exclusive clubs, and multimillion-dollar penthouses. I recall walking along the beach one morning looking up at the tops of the condominiums that lined the ocean strip. Instead of admiring the beautiful architecture, I distinctly remember the question I was asking myself over and over again: *What's wrong with me?*

Here I was in my late twenties with only a few thousand dollars in my bank account and other men at the same age were able to figure out how to become so successful that they could afford the finest sports cars and the exclusive penthouse and attract the most beautiful women. Maybe it was because they had rich parents and I lost out on the birth lottery. Many of them were in the import or export business, of which I understood very little. They were South American, Latin American, Russian, and Eastern European. It felt foreign not just in who they were but in the sense that this kind of success was simply out of my grasp—otherworldly. I was never going to have this level of wealth, and it was painful to feel that something I wanted was unattainable—but not un-attainable for others, just for me. I don't know why, but that memory, and the pain of feeling like there was something wrong with me, that there were people who had achieved success and then there were people like me, stuck with me.

Two years later I went back to South Beach. I had been getting into personal growth, learning that thoughts were things, and using tools like vision boards to begin to define what I wanted my future life to look like. And, man, was it a vision board. A $1.65 million Lamborghini Roadster, an $8.5 million penthouse in South Beach, a $75,000 Hublot Big Bang watch. It was the vision board of an up-and-coming Russian import-export oligarch, except it was mine. And here I was back on South Beach walking the exact same route looking up at the exact same penthouses.

The only problem was, I felt exactly the same way. Despite the fact that I was making a little bit more money, that I had actually upgraded my car, and that I had been spending a lot of time visualizing, the moment I glanced up at those penthouses the same tape ran inside my head. *You're never going to have that. That's for other people. There's something wrong with you. It's too expensive. You'll never have that much money or that much success.*

That second trip to Miami was a massive turning point in my understanding of transformation. The beauty of that second trip was that it was a clear, powerful reflection of where my unconscious mind and my thinking were at that time. I had done the imaginative work. I had bought into the idea that I could attain anything I could envision. I had even recorded myself screaming incantations like "abundance flows to me" and "every day in every way I'm getting wealthier and wealthier" and would listen to the recordings every day on my morning drive to work. But despite the vision boards, the books, attending the live events, the therapy, and my fundamental understanding that what I believe informs what I'm able to create in my life, Miami had shown me that I hadn't yet integrated these beliefs of abundance and possibility into my nervous system. I hadn't yet really changed my brain. How did I know? Because my reaction to the penthouse condos in Miami revealed the beliefs that were still predominant in the thought patterns of my mind. Despite all my believing, envisioning, imagining, and vision boarding, why didn't it work?

In 2006, author Rhonda Byrne published a book called *The Secret*. It was based on the idea that there is a fundamental yet undiscovered law of physics referred to as the "law of attraction" that attracts to an individual circumstances and situations similar to the thoughts that person habitually entertains. The book became an international bestseller with over thirty-five million copies sold. It gave hope to people of all economic classes, cultures, and faiths that by simply changing their thoughts they could change their lives. *The Secret* (in tandem with Napoleon Hill's *Think and Grow Rich*) motivated tens of millions of people to use their thoughts to create wealth, abundance, health, and change. And so in the first decade of the new millennium, an epidemic of imagination swept through the personal development culture, passing almost as quickly as it arrived.

One person might imagine the brand-new sports car in their driveway and post a picture of it on their desktop wallpaper. Another person might imagine their kids behaving well or getting a promotion at work or taking their dream vacation and implanting that visualization on a vision board or writing it down in their journals, reading it over and over each morning. For the vast majority of people, the car never showed up in the driveway, the kids were still misbehaving, the trip to Bora Bora never took place, and the promotion never came. Life just seemed like it wasn't accommodating this idea that what you think becomes your reality. It sounded good when you said it fast, but it simply wasn't working.

Was it that the law of attraction was a hoax? Maybe like a bad internet connection, the law broke down with so many people trying to leverage it simultaneously? Perhaps the law was being used improperly or only worked for some people sometimes. Why were so many people visualizing and imagining one thing, only to get more of the same undesired thing they had been getting for so long? Why wasn't I able to think my way into becoming a multimillion-dollar South Beach condo–owning, sports car–driving, bling-bling watch-wearing more abundant version of myself, even though I was focusing on what I wanted every day for nearly two years? The answer is pretty simple.

First, most people are simply unaware of what they actually think. At a conscious level they want more money or health or relationships or business, but at an unconscious level they believe it's not possible for them. Deciding that you're going to generate a million dollars in your business and putting it on your vision board is one thing. But identifying and transforming the limiting beliefs that are perpetuating continued cycles of stunted growth is quite another. It's not enough to simply desire a thing. One must both desire to have or be a thing and simultaneously identify and remove any psychological and emotional resistance to the actual having or being of the thing.

One person dreams of the new car but simultaneously feels like they are not worthy of it. Another individual wants the promotion but feels like she can't have it because it's a man's world. The reason why most people don't materialize change when they desire something isn't because the law of attraction doesn't work but because they haven't eliminated the predominant vibration in their nervous system that is informing Intelligence or life that "I really don't think I can have this thing." Most people are simply unaware of what they habitually think.

In other cases someone will manifest something they imagined in one area of their life. They attract the perfect soul mate but they can't seem to get out of financial insecurity. Again the cause is a lack of awareness that in the area of finance the person has some anchoring limiting beliefs. But this "works over here but not over there" type of experience leads people to believe that their thoughts create their reality sometimes but not always. That it's possible to some degree but not all degrees. This misperception creates doubt about the consistency of the law as a whole, and remember, beliefs are powerful. So those who believe that a change in their thoughts only produces a changed result "sometimes" will, well, experience just that. An inconsistency in the application of this law of attraction.

In other instances a person will "do the work" to identify what they want, perhaps even weaken or eliminate their limiting belief, and become committed to the manifestation or creation of the thing desired. But when it doesn't happen on their expected schedule, they lose faith and revert back to the old limiting belief. *Oh, this law of attraction thing doesn't really work. The change never happened.* In reality what happened is that impatience motivated the person to revert back to their old limiting beliefs before the change in their external reality could occur. Impatience is the cause of countless unmanifested changes in the lives of millions of people who were on the brink of significant change.

One of my desires for you is that you become 100 percent loyal to the idea that your thoughts, and no other factor, determine the outcomes of your life. That thoughts are things and that what you think creates your reality. We've already established this by looking at the fundamentals of behavioral psychology: what you believe determines what you think, what you feel, how you act, and therefore the results or changes that you do or do not produce in your life. But as we go deeper into your capacity to completely reengineer your reality, it's important that you understand how you are co-creating your life with Intelligence itself. You must have unshakable faith that you are a powerful creator, with no limits on your creation, and that you create first through the mind and second through action and activity.

There is no knowledge more important than to gain an understanding of how reality functions, how you can influence that reality, and a step-by-step process for changing it. Knowing how it all works will give you a foundation of faith or belief to work patiently with your inner world and your three-dimensional external world as you sculpt a new reality for yourself. We're going to build that faith, through understanding and fact, and eliminate any doubt you may have to the fundamental truth that anything is possible for you.

By now you know I love frameworks, so I'm going to framework out the nature of reality and how you can function powerfully within it. Before we do that, it's important to have a brief discussion around how thoughts become things.

How Thoughts Become Things

When I was first introduced to the idea that we have the capacity to alter and create our own reality, I was skeptical but not in total disbelief. I was open to the idea but needed to understand the details of how this could be true. How do our thoughts become things and influence the minds of others? What's really occurring on a scientific and spiritual level? What is the relationship (and is there a direct relationship) between myself and the world around me? How are we all connected, and is there really a higher intelligence that is influencing my experience of reality and actively involved in the circumstances and experiences of my life? In order for me to believe, I needed to first understand.

No doubt this need was a result of my nonreligious upbringing where there was nothing to believe in or have faith in outside the seemingly random chaos of life itself. To believe that there were fundamental laws that governed life, and that these laws were a function of a loving and intelligent design, necessitated a great amount of research, trial, error, observation, and self-experimentation. If I was going to be loyal to the laws, it was necessary for me to understand them, because I knew that if I didn't understand how it all worked, there was no way I could commit myself to the idea that I could create my own reality.

What I came to understand is that there are mathematical principles that govern our reality. Just as we have laws of physics that govern matter, its fundamental constituents, its motion and behavior through space and time, and the related entities of energy and force in order to understand how the universe behaves, so too do we have the laws of metaphysics, which according to Aristotle govern "the things transcending what is natural or physical." Metaphysics is often referred to as a philosophy of "first principles" or original causes. It is the explanation of *why* the natural world or universe functions the way it does as opposed to the explanation proposed by physics of *how* the universe functions the way it does. Metaphysics describes the functioning of consciousness or spirit and, similar to physics, is mathematical or law-based in nature.

Most of us accept reality as we experience it. We think our experience of reality is real. But it's not. Here's what I mean. In third-grade science you and I were taught that the physical stuff of the universe, matter, is composed of tiny vibrating particles known as atoms. We were shown that the atom has constituent parts, namely the nucleus (which consists of particles known as protons and neutrons) as well as a third kind of particle known as the electron, which orbits around the nucleus of the atom.

I remember a high school teacher of mine explaining the spacing and dimensions of the atom using a football field as a metaphor. He indicated that, proportionately, the nucleus of the atom would be similar to the size of a basketball placed at the fifty-yard line of a football field. The electron would be the size of a tennis ball orbiting around the parking lot. In other words, the atom itself was 99.999999 percent space or no thing and yet when we combine a bunch of these atoms into molecules and molecules combine into matter, we get very physical things like this book, your computer, your torso, the home you live in, or the highway you drive to work on. And yet each of these material things are nearly all space.

In fact what we have learned, as science has developed the capacity to view matter at an even more microscopic or quantum level, is that those parts of the atom that we believed were solid, like the neutron and electron, are only solid sometimes. At other times they are nonsolid or waveform energy. In other words, the very physical reality we experience isn't physical at all. It's a shimmering, mostly nothing, sometimes something ocean of energy. So how is it that we are able to experience such a solid, physical reality?

You've been given energetic or vibrational interpretation devices known as your senses. Your eyes are interpreting the fluctuating energies of your children into the solid-state kids that make very solid-state messes in the living room. Your ears are interpreting energy or nonsolid waveform-based vibrations into sounds. You're not actually hearing the sounds of the birds chirping or a motorcycle roaring by; you're hearing an interpretation of the energy that the birds and the motorcycles are producing. The sound isn't physical or material, it's energetic, and your auditory sensory interpretation devices are translating that vibration into a portfolio of sounds. Let's try not to complicate things further by acknowledging that the birds and the motorcycle are in fact not really there, at least in their representative physical form.

So too does your sense of taste translate vibration into flavors, your sense of smell translate energy into scents, and your sense of touch translate vibration into physical sensation. We live in a vibrating field of energy that our senses interpret into a base reality that seems very solid, very fixed, and very separate. Yet when we look beyond the interpretation of our senses, we not only see that reality isn't what it seems but it doesn't operate in ways we expect.

"Reality is an illusion albeit a persistent one."
—Albert Einstein

The Observer Effect

In 1802 physicist Thomas Young conducted an experiment that became known as the "double-slit experiment." In the experiment, Young was firing photons—tiny particles very much like electrons—through a metal plate that had two vertical slits in it. On the other side of the plate was a measuring device that would record where the photons landed. Young expected to see that some of the photons would hit the metal plate, some of them would pass through the slits, and on the other side he'd see two vertical stripes where the photons that passed through the slits would have landed on the back wall. Instead he saw what is described as an interference pattern, a series of strips along the back wall that would indicate that the photons were behaving like waves.

A good way to understand this is to imagine that Young filled the room with water and dropped a stone that caused the water to ripple through the slits rather than particles that had been fired through the slits. The waves would interact with each other on the far side of the plate, creating the interference effect on the back wall. Why were particles seemingly behaving like waves?

Young knew that when each photon left his firing device it was a particle, and he wanted to see at what point it transformed into a wave. Thinking he'd catch the transformation, he set up a recording device to watch the photons as they traveled to and through the plate. To his shock, when observing the particles during their journey from the firing device to the back wall, they behaved like particles, creating two vertical strips against the back wall. It seemed that observing the particles had an effect on how they behaved. In this case, whether they behaved like a particle or a wave. This became known as the "observer effect," which implies that observation has an impact on how the physical world, or reality, actually behaves.

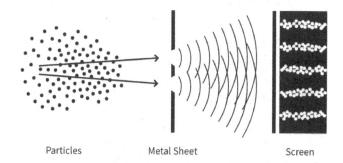

Particles   Metal Sheet   Screen

Without observation: particles behaving like waves

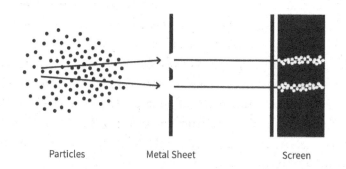

Particles   Metal Sheet   Screen

With observation: particles behaving like particles

Thomas Young's experiment is an indication that our observation and perception or beliefs about reality influence the reality that we create. Your future is a potential of many, if not infinite, possibilities. And what you believe about it determines what it will become. In other words, your life and your future can be anything, but it will absolutely be something, and the thing it will become is dependent upon what you believe about it. Each time you have a thought, you experience that thought as an emotion. That emotion emits an electrical wave-like vibration from your nervous system that, when combined with the wave-based nature of the field, collapses the potential of your life into "what is" experiences with the qualities that represent the thoughts and emotions that originated them.

What you make matter in your life becomes matter. In other words, what you believe and what you focus on in your mental space finds a way to objectify or materialize itself into your physical reality. It is as if you are mentally sculpting your reality out of a three-dimensional field of invisible clay. There is a direct correlation between you and everything around you, almost like a 360-degree virtual reality screen that is responding to your predominant thoughts and emotions. Consciousness, or the intelligent waveform potential of your life, receives your thoughts, emotions, desires, and fears and places into your reality people, places, situations, and circumstances that are designed to invoke within you the same thought or belief that originated the experience itself.

The co-creative relationship, between consciousness and you, is law-based in nature—what you think you create or attract. It is based on the specific vibrational resonance of your nervous system and calls forth matching resonances regardless of whether the experience is actually desired or feared. The only determining factor is the predominant vibration or resonance, which is a result of your predominant habit of thought or emotion. You are creating from the field via the mechanism of your thoughts and emotions, and even more remarkable is that not only are you creating from the field but you are also the field itself.

Who Are You Really?

In 2013, I had my first of now many "mystical" experiences. I had been studying both quantum and consciousness theory and became more and more interested in the possible connection between the observer effect at the quantum particle level and the idea that our thoughts and emotions have an effect on the material reality of our lives. It seemed possible, if not probable, that there existed an underlying field of energy, undetected as of yet by modern instrumentation, that underpinned our physical reality. That this field might be consciousness or awareness itself. And that the entire material world we experience might very well be originating from activities that were occurring in consciousness.

This idea, that an invisible, connective field of energy, intimately associated with what we think and feel, was the cause or origination of everything we experience in our material lives, was a theory difficult if not impossible to prove. But what I've found in my own experience, and what history has repeatedly shown, is that all great discoveries begin with intuition only later to be confirmed by logic and science, for the unknown calls forth its discovery not by clear measurement but rather by hunches and flashes of inspiration. I felt a knowingness that despite the seeming disconnection between the various elements of our physical realities—you are physically separate from another person, a tree, this book, your dog, your car—in fact everything was connected. Everything was in fact one.

For years I was bothered by this concept, that we are all one. I'd overhear conversations at my favorite vegan restaurant where new age hippies would tout the idea with little to no capacity to back it up with any kind of rational explanation. But it felt right. I remember hearing an interview at that time where Deepak Chopra, a respected thought leader on spirituality and consciousness, told Oprah Winfrey that "in the beginning," God, or All That Is, wanted to know more about itself, a quality inherent in all human beings as well, and in that desire split into two so it could now have two perspectives.

The idea that God or consciousness began as a separation struck me as untrue, and yet I had no alternative hypothesis to explain how everything in this physical world was actually one massive superorganism having an infinitely diverse and expansive experience with itself, nor where we as individuals fit into that conversation. What part or role did we play in this oneness? At the height of my inquiry into this question and after a beautiful relaxing evening with my wife, we retired to bed early, around 8:00 p.m., and then it happened.

For the next eight hours I lay in bed in a semiconscious state. I was asleep and dreaming, but I knew that I was dreaming. It was as if two parts of me were active simultaneously: my full waking self, resting with eyes closed and hands gently rested on my belly, and my lucid, dreaming self. I felt an odd, soft electrical tapping on my head as I relaxed into watching the most extraordinary scene I could possibly imagine unfold—the beginning of the universe.

In the Beginning

In the beginning I saw a light. A small speck of energy that floated far out in the distance. Around the light was a void. Nothingness. The emotions emanating from the light were some of the strongest emotions I had ever experienced. I felt love coming from the light, then compassion, and curiosity. The light felt pure and it felt alive. There was a single moment, as the emotions were building, when I felt tremendous desire, curiosity, and wonder.

In the peak of that emotion there was a great flash, and the light expanded across the void in every direction. Along with the flash, there was an overwhelming feeling of desire coming from the light that I experienced as a deep desire to know more about itself, about life, about what there was to discover "out there."

The light expanded, and as it did, it created space, distinct from the void. In 360 degrees the light expanded and pushed the void out to the edges of its expansion. It was as if I was looking at the universe, or outer space, born from the expansion of the light, with nothing yet in it. As the light continued to expand it reached a point where it could no longer push into the outer edges of the void and began to retract toward the center from which it originated. I saw distinctly that there were two different forms of this light wave energy. One wave of the light energy was an outward form, pushing the outer limits of space into the void—an outward arch. The other wave of energy was the energy that was returning from the outer limits of the expansion. Two energy waves of identical and opposite form, crossing and meeting each other, as one life.

In that moment, when the outward arch met the inward arch, the yin met the yang, the male met the female, something miraculous emerged. In the swirling intersection of the two waves I saw that spin or torque began to occur. Like two currents in a river that catch each other and create a small whirlpool, the opposing energies danced for a moment, intertwined together. And from that union of two waves crossing each other I saw the emergence of something new. I saw a particle. One microscopic piece of matter that emerged from the nothingness of the energy of life itself. I then watched as the entire physical universe emerged. First atoms, then molecules, space dust, light, larger chunks of matter, rocks, asteroids, planets, comets, suns, moons, solar systems, galaxies—the entire material universe emerged from this fluctuating field of energy that had created the platform for the material universe to become real. A single no thing that gave rise to the everything.

In his book *Sapiens: A Brief History of Humankind*, author Yuval Noah Harari presents a brilliant scientific explanation of what happened after the universe came into existence. His observation combined with my mystical moment helped to complete a full picture of how we are all connected as One, the metaphysical implications of that connection, and the source of our true identity or spirithood. Harari explains that approximately 13.5 billion years ago, physics was born. Before that time there was no physics because there was no thing. There was no time, matter, energy, or space. Harari doesn't suggest what there was prior to this moment but acknowledges that some phenomenon occurred after which physics as we know it today came into existence.

What I'm suggesting is that prior to this moment in fact there was no thing that existed. What existed was unembodied life itself. A universal intelligence without a body yet to enliven. Source energy that had not yet manifested into any kind of material form. The no thing that is the underlying foundation or cause of everything. Harari goes on to explain that three hundred million years after physics emerged, chemistry formed. All that stuff created out of the waveform interactions of All That Is or Intelligence cooled down and coalesced into molecules. The material stuff now had a distinctness as it intelligently organized itself into the elements of the periodic table. Chemistry, given nearly ten billion years more, recombined and evolved into biology or life-forms.

How did a material universe with no visible life all of a sudden become propagated with life-forms? The answer seems to be that time lends to diversity and complexity. Over ten billion years as chemistry evolved into more diverse physical and material structures, some of those structures developed the ability to receive life into them. Inanimate objects evolved into "life-forms." In other words, substructures similar to receivers or antennas, far distant forms of today's brain, developed inside inanimate objects so they could receive life or consciousness into them in order to become alive—to enable nonphysical consciousness or intelligence to have a physical experience.

This moment hallmarks a major milestone in the evolution of consciousness where that which formed out of consciousness could actually now receive consciousness back into itself. Consciousness could now embody itself and have a physical experience of life. Nearly 4 billion years after the appearance of life-forms, an organism known as the human being emerged. This occurred only 2.5 million years ago. Of several varietals of human there was one that entered the scene just 70,000 years ago, *Homo sapiens*, which has now become the dominant species on this planet and as of yet the most advanced of all conscious expression that has been identified.

Not only is the human being capable of receiving consciousness and acting as a vehicle for the expression of pure intelligence into the world, but it developed a particularly unique brain structure that afforded itself the ability to communicate using complex language, to imagine, and to become aware of its own awareness. In that, humans have developed the unique ability to change their minds and therefore reengineer their own neural circuitry. Intelligence, consciousness, God, soul, spirit, or whatever your preferred nomenclature is to describe the "One" now inhabited a biological species that had the ability to do what Intelligence had achieved in the beginning—to create something from nothing using thought, emotion, and desire and to discover more of its true nature via its inter-action and response to that which it created. Not just individually but in tandem with seven billion other humans connected to each other and to the superorganism itself. One intelligence having infinite experiences and growing and evolving through the interactions of all its parts.

> "Rather than produced by the brain, consciousness may be a fundamental force of the universe, like gravity or mass. In this way, consciousness came into being when the universe began, and exists everywhere and in everything."
> —David Chalmers

Why is this important to understand? Because you don't wake up each morning in acknowledgment that you are a powerful creator gifted with the same extraordinary capabilities and possibilities as creation itself. You do not consciously acknowledge on a moment-by-moment basis that your thoughts and emotions are being received by all of consciousness and that all of life is conspiring to fulfill on your predominant thoughts and desires. You have developed a personality that inflicts massive limitation on who you believe you are, what you are or are not capable of, and these restrictions create suffering and limit the achievement of your full potential. To become your own unique expression of Intelligence itself and close the gap between the individual you and the great body of intelligence, intuition, and genius that is trying to work through you, you must give up your old identity and don a new one that contains within it the inherent acknowledgment that anything is possible for you and that all of life is working for your greatest growth, your greatest prosperity, and your greatest evolution.

You are IT, and it is having an experience as YOU. And in light of this awareness and new identity, in tandem with the tools you have to rewire your own brain, you can realign your thoughts, emotions, and personality with who you really are—an individual expression of the most powerful, unstoppable, creative force that has ever existed, the creator of life itself.

> **"Consciousness exists as a kind of field, outside the brain, and the function of the brain is to "pick up" consciousness, like a radio receiver, and then to "channel" it into our individual organism."**
> —Robert Forman

One of the most powerful moments in scripture is the moment when Moses meets the Burning Bush. Moses has been living his limited personhood his entire life. Abandoned at birth as a Hebrew boy, adopted by Pharaoh's daughter, raised as Egyptian royalty, everything about Moses's life was inauthentic. In sensing that inauthenticity and his connection to the Hebrew slaves, Moses kills an Egyptian slave master and is exiled to tend sheep for the rest of his life in the desert. While tending to his herd one day, Moses comes upon the Burning Bush, representing among many things his Spiritual Vision or greatness. The Bush tells Moses of his destiny, that he must return to Pharaoh and demand the freedom of the Hebrew slaves and lead them to a promised land. Moses, perplexed as one would imagine by this talking fiery plant, asks who it is he is speaking with.

For the first time God reveals his name, Yahweh, which translates into "I am that I am." Moses is having a conversation with the Intelligence or God within him, the purest essence of his spirit. Without the labels, the limitations, the childhood stories, the beliefs, the purest essence of who Moses is, the pure intelligence of spirit, calls Moses forth to his dharma.

That same I AM essence of Intelligence that was Moses is the same intelligence or spirit that is the life force within all living things and also the vibrational underpinning of the entire material world. All interconnected through an invisible matrix of consciousness, what Aristotle, Plato, the Buddhists, Taoists, Hindus, and Christians referred to as a luminiferous ether, great, shining, beyond and amidst this world, the spirit in man, with no beginning and no end. This is your true nature, nothing less.

Your reality is a holographic experience reflecting back to you your own thoughts, beliefs, emotions, programs, and personality through the experiences you create. Your reaction to the experiences you've created informs you of you, who you are, and what you believe. All of us are producers of our own personal movies while simultaneously serving as actors and characters in someone else's. Together we create one single epic that is tied together by each of our individual stories. To navigate this collective reality elegantly and powerfully, you must understand how you operate as a character in the system and how the system itself functions. The work that we have done together up until this point forms the basis of this great understanding.

In the following sections, we will put all the pieces together into a framework for living powerfully, for becoming a Phenomenon, for learning how to create what you want and how to transform the beliefs and programs inside you when you realize you've created something that you *don't* want. To use this multidimensional field of intelligence to elevate you out of suffering and raise your consciousness to a new level of abundance, impact, joy, freedom, and spiritual enlightenment. To close the gap between your present reality and the infinite potential that you are an extension and part of.

15

The Higher Power System

As I was understanding these laws of the universe more, I wanted to put them to the test. I decided to run an experiment that pushed the limits of my beliefs. I knew I had some more work to do around my beliefs regarding money, and I realized that I had put a cap on my ability to earn income based on how much money I was making in my business at that time. It was a business backed by investors, and we weren't making a profit yet so the only income I could make was my salary. Effectively I was an employee.

The experiment looked something like this: I decided that by the end of the year I was going to make an additional $60,000 of income from a source (or sources) outside of my business. In many ways this felt impossible, which is precisely why I chose it. I didn't have any investments, I had around $20,000 in my bank account, I was upside down on my primary home and two rental properties, and I couldn't see any reasonable way at the time that I'd be able to generate that kind of income outside of my job.

But at that point I had also come to understand a few things. First, that I didn't need to know "the how." Second, that if I made a decision, I would start to have thoughts and ideas and see opportunities to produce the additional $60,000. And lastly, and perhaps most importantly, that the moment I could truly believe this was possible, an intelligent power

176

far greater than myself would conspire to create the circumstances and situations necessary to realize my goal. It was April 1, 2014, when I made the decision.

Two weeks later my friend Dan invited me to lunch. He wanted me to meet his client Roland, who owned a mortgage brokerage company out of Tampa, Florida. I was in the mortgage lead-generation business, and Dan thought there might be an opportunity to broker a deal. As it turned out, Roland wasn't just a mortgage broker but an entrepreneur with a portfolio of companies, some of them in the internet marketing space, which gave us a number of topics to relate to each other on.

During the lunch, I shared with Roland that I had been in twelve-step recovery for several years and that when I first got into it, my therapist had me commit to abstaining from drugs, alcohol, sex, and smoking for the first ninety days. My friend Dan, while not an addict, participated in what we dubbed "the ninety-day challenge" with me and shared that those ninety days of clean living had really transformed his outlook and experience of life. The lunch was enjoyable, and I hadn't given it another thought until I received a phone call from Roland about a month later.

"I wanted to thank you," he said. "What you shared about your recovery inspired me, and I haven't had a drink in thirty days." Unbeknownst to me, Roland had been struggling with alcohol and now had thirty days of sobriety under his belt. "I'd love for you to come down to Tampa so I can thank you and take you to lunch." A week later I drove the hour from Orlando to Tampa and arrived about thirty minutes early for my appointment with Roland. His secretary ushered me into his office and offered me a seat on the sofa in the back of the room as he wrapped up a meeting. He gave me a brief nod of acknowledgment and continued the discussion with the two young men who sat in front of him.

I listened for the good part of fifteen minutes as the two men in their late twenties pitched Roland on an online marketing idea that happened to be in my realm of expertise. After the meeting he and I headed out to lunch at a local ritzy restaurant. We discussed what it was like over the last thirty days and how his life was dramatically improving as a result of his abstinence from alcohol. Then he asked me a question.

"That idea those guys had. That's in your realm of expertise, isn't it?"

"Yeah, it is," I replied. "I had tried something similar a few years earlier, in fact."

"What do you think about their idea now?" he asked.

"I think it's solid. It addresses the challenges I ran into, and the opportunity is even greater now than before. You know, sometimes you're just a little too early with an idea." I laughed. "I think the timing is right for what they're doing." We finished our lunch and I headed back to Orlando. That night I received a phone call from Roland.

"Listen, I've negotiated to invest $40,000 in that idea this morning for ownership of half of the company. I have a proposition for you."

I listened.

"If you want to invest $20,000, you can take half of my half. The only catch is that I want you coming to Tampa once a week to actively work in the business. Those guys are really inexperienced, and they're going to need a little bit of guidance. What do you say?"

I was really attracted to the business model they had put together. The cash flowed quickly. It was already making over $100,000 a month with little to no expenses. It had the opportunity to quickly scale to over a million a month without much more investment. At the same time, $20,000 was literally all I had to my name. If I invested the money, I wouldn't have anything left to backstop me in case something went wrong. But I was also learning that if I wanted to create more in my life, I couldn't be making decisions out of fear. I was nervous, but I agreed.

"Okay, I'm in," I said. "When do we need me to start coming down to Tampa?"

"Next week," he replied.

It was now midsummer. I was spending four days a week on my primary business in Orlando and one day driving to Tampa to work with the two young guys, who turned out to be brothers. They were difficult to work with. One was a nightclub owner; both were alcoholics and clearly using drugs on a regular basis. It was nearly impossible to bring order to their business, if you could even call it that. They had basically figured out how to spend a few thousand dollars on online marketing and quickly turn it around for a fifty times return. But if the business was going to scale to the level that my partner and I envisioned, it was going to need systems, processes, and good people—none of which existed at the moment and all of which the two brothers were highly resistant to.

The summer passed, and in the fall I started to see cracks in the model. Ad costs were increasing, we were failing to deliver on our product, and new team members came on board without any training or direction and quickly became dissatisfied and quit. We were experiencing a high level of employee turnover, and there was nothing on the horizon that would lead me to believe the brothers were going to be open to implementing any of the many improvement suggestions I had made. I frequently found myself spending the entire day in arguments with them and putting out fires that could have been easily prevented. In late October, I got a phone call from the older brother.

"Look, man, it's no secret that we don't get along. We're not happy. I know you're not happy. Why don't you let us propose something to buy you out?" he asked.

I wasn't sure what the proposal was going to look like. Most of our conversations had been about making millions, but the last few months had grown stagnant. At this point I was open to anything. A few weeks later around mid-November they sent over the initial term sheet, which was a little less than what I was willing to accept. Over the next month we went back and forth in negotiation and finally came to agreement. On December 27 I sold my shares back to the brothers and they wired the buyout amount to my bank account according to the terms established.

I got my $20,000 investment back, plus $60,000. Three days before the end of 2014. Exactly the amount I decided I would make by the end of the year, from a source that had nothing to do with my primary business.

How It Works

If thoughts become things and create our reality, and if reality is corresponding to what you think, there can be perhaps no undertaking more worthwhile than to understand the mechanism by which our thinking is interfacing with reality. There is a system at work that is based on mathematical principles or laws. It is as unfailing in its predictability as gravity. It is as consistent as the sun rising. Understanding this system will allow you to not only engage productively and intelligently with it, but it will also afford you the opportunity to use the experiences of your life to become even more deeply aware of your limiting or empowering beliefs so that you can reengineer your inner attitude and produce dramatic changes in your external reality.

Everything we've covered so far—the foundations, awareness, philosophies, distinctions, and tools—have been the building blocks for understanding how consciousness, or infinite intelligence, systematically operates both around us, with us, and through us. Your true nature is that of a powerful creator, and your purpose is (as suggested in the Big Book of Alcoholics Anonymous) to be *"an intelligent agent, a spearhead of God's ever advancing Creation."* The following is the manual for how your life and reality actually work—what I call the Higher Power System. The diagram below is a simple but powerful visual representation of how that system functions.

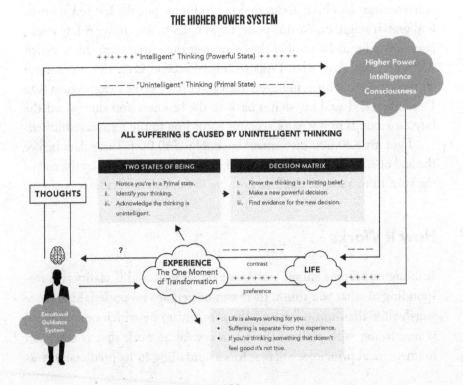

THE HIGHER POWER SYSTEM

+ + + + + + "Intelligent" Thinking (Powerful State) + + + + + +

— — — — "Unintelligent" Thinking (Primal State) — — — —

Higher Power Intelligence Consciousness

ALL SUFFERING IS CAUSED BY UNINTELLIGENT THINKING

TWO STATES OF BEING	DECISION MATRIX
i. Notice you're in a Primal state.	i. Know the thinking is a limiting belief.
ii. Identify your thinking.	ii. Make a new powerful decision.
iii. Acknowledge the thinking is unintelligent.	iii. Find evidence for the new decision.

THOUGHTS

EXPERIENCE
The One Moment of Transformation

contrast

+ + + + + + +

LIFE

+ + + + +

preference

Emotional Guidance System

- Life is always working for you.
- Suffering is separate from the experience.
- If you're thinking something that doesn't feel good it's not true.

Your true nature is consciousness itself. The life or spirit that enlivens you is the same one spirit that expresses itself through all creation. You are a truly unique expression of that infinite Intelligence, providing a critical perspective that allows for the ongoing expansion and evolution of consciousness and the universe, via the mechanism of your own life. You are critically important, unique, and special and yet no more so than any other person or creature. We are all making a great contribution toward the ongoing evolution of creation itself through the living of our own individual and unique lives. This is you, represented in the bottom left of the Higher Power System diagram above.

On a moment-by-moment basis you are thinking, observing, believing, and making judgments about life. You are having thoughts about your experiences in the past, present, and future, or even having thoughts about your own thoughts. You are thinking you aren't good enough, or that success is inevitable, that you look good today, that something bad may happen in the future, that you shouldn't have said something you said or that you need to lose weight but can't because you're an undisciplined person. The activation of these thoughts is the activation of neural networks, and that electrical vibration in your brain—which can be measured using modern scientific technologies—is emitted into your external environment just as a light bulb emits light toward its surroundings.

Each time you have one of your daily six thousand thoughts, you are communicating or transmitting vibration or energy into a collective vibrational reality from both your brain and your nervous system, and that energy will eventually, through the mechanism of consciousness, make its way into the materialization of a physical experience. The idea, or word, will become flesh, or physical. With each thought you are contributing, shaping, and sculpting the collective consciousness that manifests itself as the day-to-day experiences of your life. Those experiences usually involve others, and as such we are co-creating our reality not only with the field of consciousness or Intelligence itself but also with each other as embodied agents of consciousness.

Using Your Emotional Guidance System

When you have thoughts that are aligned with the mathematical laws of consciousness, meaning your interpretation of your life or your past or your present experience is that life is working for your greatest growth, greatest prosperity, and greatest evolution, you feel good. You feel good because your brain and nervous system are producing a vibration that is resonant with the vibration of reality itself. These are intelligent thoughts, in alignment with the structure of Intelligence, and as a result your nervous system maintains itself in a parasympathetic and restful or Powerful state. From this state you are connected and in flow with consciousness, or life, or God, and in that alignment you are vibrant, energized, resourceful, intuitive, compassionate, peaceful, and joyous. Thoughts produced from this state are materializing into future experiences that, when you experience them, will invoke the same kind of Powerful states from you.

In other words, joyful thoughts create joyful experiences, peaceful thoughts produce peaceful experiences, and abundant thoughts create abundant experiences into your future. For the purposes of illustration I've marked these aligned, resonate, intelligent thoughts with a plus in the Higher Power System diagram above—not to imply any kind of judgment of good or bad but simply to distinguish them from dissonant Primal thoughts and to indicate that they are of a higher frequency or vibration than their counterparts.

When you entertain thoughts that are dissonant with the true or mathematical nature of reality, when you perceive something as a problem, or when you become afraid that something in your life is or will go "wrong" or that you will fail (which is not an actual possibility in an intelligently architected love- and growth-driven reality), you produce a dissonant vibration, and you experience that dissonance as a Primal state of being. You move into the sympathetic activation of your nervous system and experience fight, flight, fear, freeze, or some other form of suffering as a result of the dissonance of these "unintelligent thoughts."

These feelings are a signal from your emotional guidance system, or nervous system, that your thoughts are simply out of alignment. They are misinterpretations of what is *really* taking place. A misinterpretation of what is real. As you think these thoughts, you emit into the collective consciousness, or field, a dissonant vibration that begins to realize itself into future experiences, situations, and circumstances that, when you experience them, will invoke a Primal state from you. Thoughts of worry produce experiences that invoke worry. Thoughts of jealousy create future situations that will cause you to be jealous. What you feel in the moment is creating a future that will feel the same way. The time between the thought and the actual experience is simply the gestation period for the conception of that idea. This is part of the process of how thoughts become things and how ideas become alive.

How Thoughts Become Things

The process of materialization, as beliefs take physical form or become matter, begins as all of consciousness, Intelligence, or what I also refer to as Higher Power (as marked in the top right of the diagram), receives this vibrational or energetic transmission from you. People, situations, and circumstances begin to respond to create coincidences and synchronicities based upon your predominant thought vibration. The entirety of consciousness receives your mental and emotional request, and with the passage of time, the thought itself will materialize, objectify, or realize itself into your experience as your life. As you meet these manifested experiences, they will invoke the same emotion from you that initiated the entire process.

When you experience something you like, it is an experience of "preference." When you experience something you don't like, it is an experience of "contrast." Powerful, good-feeling, aligned, and intelligent thoughts create preferred life experiences that are both desired and feel good. Primal, bad-feeling, misaligned, and unintelligent thoughts create contrasting experiences that create undesired experiences and feel bad. The intelligent person understands that their experiences are not the cause of their thoughts and emotions but rather the effect of them. Our thoughts and emotions catalyze the materialization of our experiences, and we can change the experiences of our life by transforming our habits of thinking and feeling—by transforming our beliefs.

**The intelligent person understands
that their experiences are not the
cause of their thoughts and emotions
but rather the effect of them.**

The beauty of the structure of the system is that your life or life situation can always be changed. If you are repeatedly creating experiences you don't prefer, you can change your thoughts and therefore change your results. And it is in the moment of your reaction to an experience you do not like, the experience of contrast, that you can apply the tools and technologies you've learned so far to create permanent and dramatic change. All transformation takes place in one moment, as marked in the Higher Power System diagram—the moment you experience that which you've created. Here's how this works.

Using the Methodology: Doing the Work

Let's imagine you are having an undesired experience. Perhaps it's a medical bill that arrives that requires you to pay more than you expected and so you become worried. Perhaps you're late for work and first need to drop the kids off at school and they aren't complying with your requests to get ready and you begin to feel overwhelmed. Maybe you're having a physical discomfort or pain you've been living with for a while and it scares you. In that moment, in the midst of the experience, is the one moment of transformation. The opportunity to transform your beliefs and create a different future. *The key here is to simply notice that you don't feel good. That you've moved into a Primal state. This is Step 1.*

From here it's important to remember that the experience itself isn't actually causing your suffering or emotional discomfort. Note the key

distinctions in the Higher Power System. These are crucial understandings that you can bring into the moment to support the transformation
or shift. The feelings you are having are separate from the experience
itself. And your feelings are caused by one thing and one thing only: the
thoughts you are having about the experience. Said another way, your
belief about the experience. Perhaps you're thinking that you're not going
to have enough money to pay the bill or make it through the end of the
month, or that you're never going to get out of financial insecurity. Maybe
you're thinking that the kids will never listen to you and you're never
going to be able to get it all done today and therefore you're a failure as
a parent. Perhaps the physical pain has been with you so long that you
believe it will never go away or that you will never be able to experience
the full joy you want out of life as a result of it. *Step 2 is to identify the
thinking while knowing it is the thinking, not the experience itself, that is
causing you to move into a Primal state.*

Once you've identified the thinking that is causing you to be in a
Primal state, it's important to acknowledge that all thinking that creates
suffering—whether it be boredom, overwhelm, anxiety, jealousy, anger,
or fear—is unintelligent. Anytime you move into a Primal state, it is a
result of *untrue thinking*. In other words, the thinking or meaning you're
giving the situation simply isn't in alignment with what's real or the nature of the loving, abundant, law-based nature of reality. *Step 3 is simply
an acknowledgment that if you're thinking something that doesn't feel good,
it must not be true.* Your nervous system is indicating that the thoughts
you're having about the situation are dissonant, and you experience that
dissonance as negative emotion. Now that you've been able to identify
the thinking and you acknowledge that the thinking isn't true (even
though it may still feel true for you in the moment), you can move on
to the next step.

Step 4 is to work the Decision Matrix. Now that you've identified the
limiting belief, which doesn't feel good, isn't congruent with what you're
wanting to create and is untrue, you can leverage the Power of Decision
to realign yourself to the experience. Remember, beliefs are decisions,
and you have an ability to transform your experience of the situation by

simply making a new decision. What decision should you make? Well, one that is more in alignment with what you want. And if your belief about this experience isn't true, then some form of the opposite must be true. That new decision will feel good because it is true.

New Empowered Decisions

You can receive an unexpected bill and still decide that you have enough, you've always had enough, and you will always have enough to provide for yourself. After all, it's true, isn't it? Take it a step further and you can decide that even more abundance is coming your way, and the only reason you don't have the wealth and financial freedom you desire yet is because you've been operating through the lens of your limited money beliefs. That's all changing now as a result of your new awareness and your ability to change your mind.

Yes, things may feel hectic with the kids, but you can make a decision that your kids *are* listening to you; it's just that they don't show it very well because, well, they're kids. Decide that these are the precious albeit chaotic magical moments that you'll never get back and that you don't need to get it all done. That anything you don't get done didn't need to get done today and everything seems to resolve, over time, on its own. That life is supporting you in making it all work. After all, that is what your experience has been, for the most part. Isn't it?

Perhaps this medical condition or pain has been with you for a while, but you can decide that the body has the capacity to heal itself (and it simply hasn't because you had been so focused on having the pain for the rest of your life), or that you can still enjoy your life while experiencing the physical pain or discomfort and that the only real problem is your worry about the pain, not the pain itself.

Each of these new decisions feel better than the limiting beliefs, and they feel better because they're *actually more true*. These experiences aren't creating these reactions or beliefs but rather the beliefs have been around for most of your life and have been manufacturing more of these experiences. You've always felt like you were financially insecure, or that you couldn't get it all done, or that something was going to prevent you from fully enjoying your life. The bill, the kids, the pain—they are simply the current moment's manifestation of those beliefs, and in the moment of experiencing that which you have been unconsciously and repetitively creating you have an opportunity to break the cycle by, in the moment, changing your reaction to it.

When you make a new decision you alter your perception. You experience the experience differently. That change in your perception is a change in your brain. That change in your brain transforms the frequency of vibration and your habit of thought moving forward, and that change begins to manifest itself as new experiences that contain more of what you want and less of what you don't.

In the moment you doubt financial security, you make a new decision that invokes abundance. In the moment you are overwhelmed, you make a new decision that brings calm. And in the moment you are fearful, you make a new decision that brings peace. You retrain your nervous system and your mind by using the tools from this book to become someone different in that moment, thereby translating the experience into a higher vibrational interpretation of the experience, which you experience as a Powerful state. As you experience that moment differently, the brain records it, old neural networks begin to fade away, and new ones are forged.

You don't become an abundant, calm, peaceful person by trying to control the uncontrollable experiences around you. You become the abundant, calm, peaceful person by thinking abundant, calm, peaceful thoughts and as a result produce an abundant, calm, peaceful future instead of the cycle of suffering that had become habit. You metabolize the habitual experience through the lens of an elevated, intelligent perspective and through that process raise your consciousness to a higher, more intelligent level. From this new perspective, all problems can be solved.

"We can't solve problems by using the same kind of thinking we used when we created them."

—Albert Einstein

Finding the Evidence

The last piece of this transformative process is to reinforce the new deci-sion by asking yourself: *What evidence do I have for the fact that this new decision is true? What evidence do I have for the fact that I have always had enough and that I have enough now and that I will always have enough?* Well, one piece of evidence is that it's fundamentally true, isn't it? Perhaps you don't have as much as you would like, but that's a very different thing than having this idea that you don't have enough. You're still here, which by default must mean you've always had enough!

What evidence do I have for the fact that my kids listen to me, and that these are the magic moments, and that I don't need to get it all done, I just need to get done what I can get done? Your kids certainly listen to you when it's time for ice cream, don't they? Have you ever really been able to get it all done? That's kind of an absurd notion, isn't it? (And a stressful one.) Haven't you always found a way to prioritize the must-do's and get them done? And when you weren't able to accomplish certain things as expected, did the world come crashing down around you? Of course not. The real issue is that the fear that it will is causing you to be stressed around your kids, which adds more stress to the situation. The new decision is intelligent, meaning it's even more aligned with what's true, and when you take a moment to slow down and evaluate your own thinking, you'll find it's actually what you believe.

Is that pain going to prohibit you from the joy you want to have in your life? Well, certainly if you keep worrying it will. But aren't there times when you've had the discomfort and enjoyed your life too? Aren't the times of greatest discomfort when you've focused on a limited future as a result of the pain, not the pain in the present moment itself? Doesn't the pain get worse when you are in a stressful, suffering, Primal state? Isn't it possible that the only thing preventing your healing is the fact that you're maintaining a state of distress? Is it possible that if you could just accept your pain without the story or limiting beliefs, your body might move into a healing state? It's not difficult to find evidence for the fact that your new decision is true if you are patient and willing to explore it.

As you now perceive your present experience differently, from a Powerful state, that change in perception is a change in your brain. You record the new experience with new thoughts and emotions, as a result of the new decision, and you overwrite the old memory and habit of reaction. As a result, you are now more inclined to perceive the next similar experience through the lens of your new decision. What's more, from that moment forward, you are putting off a different vibration as a result of a changed mind. Your habitual thoughts and emotions change. You've converted an experience of contrast into an experience of preference. And so the cycle continues. We begin again in the bottom left of the Higher Power System diagram, with you. Your new way of thinking and feeling begins to create and attract improved experiences. And, with each new experience, you are more inclined to view the experience through the lens of your new decisions. Over time, the old limiting beliefs are pruned, and as you materialize a new reality from your new personality, you reengineer both your reality and yourself.

16

Laws of the System

All experiences are simply a reflection of your consciousness. When you make a new decision you change your perception. And as you change your perception you change your beliefs and your brain. From that moment on you begin to think differently about the challenge or situation. As a result, the challenge or situation, given enough time, must change too.

Another way to understand this is to realize that each new present moment is the manifestation of a memory. Because the brain is a goal-achieving machine and because your thoughts create vibration that life corresponds to in the form of situations, circumstances, coincidences, and synchronicities, you will continue to create experiences that map to your belief systems and your past until you change your beliefs. The financial insecurity you are experiencing now is simply a memory of the financial insecurity you observed as a child. The experience of stress, overwhelm, and not being able to get it all done that you're experiencing with your kids and your schedule is simply a memory of those same beliefs and emotions that were formed when you were a kid, playing themselves out in a present-moment manifestation. That fear that something will threaten the joy of your life that has shown up in the form of a physical pain is simply a present-moment manifestation of the memory of an original experience in your childhood that shaped your perception and belief system way back then. The new experience affords you an opportunity to forge a new path forward.

Oftentimes, as you use the Two States of Being and the Decision Matrix to transform your current experience (or *after* an experience as you use the methodology to transform it in the recent past), you'll see that the meaning you gave the situation or circumstance decades ago was *also* unintelligent. You were never not good enough; your parents just didn't have the capacity to express their full love for you. People weren't untrustworthy; you simply experienced one situation where someone betrayed your trust (while ignoring the thousands of instances that people honored it). You didn't actually do it all on your own; you had lots of help, but a few isolated and misunderstood incidences and the meaning you gave them shaped a trajectory of experiences that seemed like people never did things right and if you wanted it done right you had to do it yourself.

In the present moment, as you engage with the experiences you've co-created with Infinite Intelligence, you're afforded an opportunity to transform your present perception and beliefs, which simultaneously changes your perception of your past and the quality of your future. Each moment you are recording the experiences of your life along with the meaning you are giving it. As you record the same kind of experience through a different meaning, belief, or perception, you overwrite the old belief system, which creates an actual neurophysiological change in your brain.

You become the new belief and you create future experiences that reinforce that new belief. By noticing how you feel, identifying when you've moved into a Primal state, and using the methodology to work through the moment, you heal the misunderstandings of your limiting belief, change your brain, and radically alter your present and future life.

Not every experience is a disliked or unwanted experience. Many of your experiences are enjoyable or preferences. These experiences are manifestations of your *empowered* beliefs: that you *are* good enough, that abundance *is* your natural birthright, that things *don't* have to be hard, and that help and resources *are* always on the way. When you experience these desired situations and circumstances, you can use them to deepen your empowered beliefs or decisions through gratitude and appreciation.

As you express gratitude and appreciation, you are increasing your focus on the thing desired. As you increase your focus, you strengthen the myelin around the memory of these experiences and the meanings and beliefs associated with them. You train your nervous system to respond with a Powerful state more often. As you build stronger networks, you are more likely to interpret other situations or circumstances similarly. As you are grateful, you find and create more circumstances and situations to be grateful for. Gratitude directs both the unconscious mind and life to conspire together to create more of that which you appreciate. Want a bank account you love? Love the bank account you have. Want a relationship you love? Find ways to love the relationship you have. Want a business you love? Love the business you have. If you want a life you love, the fastest way to create it is to love the life you have.

Want a life you love, love the life you have.

It's also important to acknowledge when you see the system responding to the changes within you. Faith in the Higher Power System is an essential aspect of freeing yourself from your limiting beliefs and suffering and having a powerful living experience. Because your beliefs inform and create your experience of reality, believing in the system is essential. To that extent it's helpful to acknowledge the system when you observe it performing according to law. Acknowledge that you are creating something you don't prefer, do the work, and then recognize when your perceptions, thoughts, ideas, and the actual manifestations of your life transform. The system allows you to create through the power of Intelligence itself rather than the misperception that you are at the whim of a random, chaotic, and oftentimes unloving universe.

To be in observation, awe, and appreciation of the Higher Power System itself will bring an even greater awareness that will allow you to participate with the system in easier, more effortless ways. In a sense your deepening awareness of the system itself will begin to train your nervous system to operate within and with the system at an automatic and unconscious level. The more you see the system working, the more the system works for you.

When my students first learn the Higher Power System they have many questions. Once they start applying it to their life they have even more. *Why do I keep experiencing the same things I don't prefer even when I think I've changed my beliefs? How do other people's beliefs and lives impact my own life? In a loving system, why do bad things happen? If a Higher Power really loves me, why did I have trauma in my life? Why do I have limiting beliefs at all?* This section addresses key distinctions of the system and answers commonly asked questions in an effort to deepen your understanding, faith in, and application of everything we've discussed so far.

A Spiritual Practice

Applying the methodology is a spiritual practice. You are being called to a more spiritual life—a life where you are more consistently connected to spirit or Higher Power and acting freely as a unique expression of Intelligence as opposed to reacting to your past experiences, programs, and traumas. This life is inevitable as you dishabituate the primal brain from the thoughts and emotions associated with it.

The primal brain is instinctive, not expansive, creative, or enlightened. The ability to use the experiences of your own life along with an awareness of your own thoughts and emotions to transform the programs that drive your limiting beliefs and suffering is an act of self-evolution. You are transforming those unintelligently functioning parts of you into intelligence and in the process are creating a new capacity to deepen your connection with yourself and with everything around you.

Your bond with spirit grows as you increase your alignment and connection to your higher self—resulting in a greater expression of your genius and, over time, the achievement of your full potential. This work offers a framework for living a spiritual life—being in the act or condition of spirit. There is nothing more important than a commitment to a spiritual life. Deepening your connection with spirit is the cause. Greater health, wealth, relationships, clarity, purpose, and impact is the effect.

The System Is Law-Based and Agnostic

You know what you want, whether it's more ease, greater joy, more financial abundance, freedom of time, intimate relationships, deepening of your spirituality, or more material things. So why would life give you something you don't want? It's a great question. The Higher Power System is agnostic in the sense that it "assumes" you want what you put your consistent attention and focus on. In its perfection, the system isn't designed to give you what you want but what you think and feel. The system is designed to continue to push us through to expansion, growth, and evolution—one of the fundamentally scientific and metaphysical qualities of the universe and all life within it. While life is agnostic to what you want, it is fully committed to manifesting what you believe. It is a living software system whose code runs everything from the health of the body, to the interconnectedness of schools of fish and flying birds, to the great intelligence of the biosphere and the perfect coordination of the orbits and gravitational pulls of the cosmos. There is never a flaw in the system, only a flaw in our understanding of it.

By supporting the realization of what it is you unconsciously think and feel on a moment-by-moment basis rather than what you desire in a wishful moment, the system is designed to elevate your awareness of yourself through the repetitive quality of the experiences of your life. For each and every one of us there was a moment when we finally said, "No more! I can't take one more instant of this. Not one more time!" It is in these moments of deciding, or in a sense surrendering, that you open yourself to the possibility that you cannot continue to be the same way and expect different results. The system leans on you until you acquiesce, and through that loving pressure you become willing to become something or someone different. That someone different is your true self and your full potential. Who you are destined to become. If life gave you what you wished for rather than giving you reflections of who you are, you would have no mechanism by which to grow and evolve, both of which are the greatest joys and accomplishments that we all ultimately and innately desire.

> **"For whosoever hath, to him shall be given, and he shall have more abundance: but whosoever hath not, from him shall be taken away even that he hath."**
> —Matthew 13:12 (KJV)

The Bible passage in Matthew speaks to this perpetual nature of the system. The first time I read this passage I thought it supremely unfair. Those who don't have will have less but those who do have will have more? How could that be a governing law of a loving and generous universe? When you understand the mechanics of the Higher Power System, it makes perfect sense. If you have a lack mentality you will continue to create experiences that reflect your scarcity mindset. And if you don't do something to change your mindset in the one moment of transformation, the moment you interact with the experience you've created, you will deepen and perpetuate those beliefs.

Over time a momentum is created, which will strip you of nearly everything you have in order to glaringly reflect back to you the unintelligent psychological causes originating from within. The good news is that momentum can be changed by simply making a new decision and finding evidence for the fact that abundance is and always has been your birthright. That money flows to those who decide it shall flow to them and that the only reason you haven't been living as abundant a life as you desire is because of a simple misunderstanding called a limiting belief. Once you change your mind you change your life, and a new momentum is created. Matthew articulates this new momentum when he says that "he who hath, to him even more shall be given."

The system is mathematical and precise in nature. The laws that govern reality and creation are scientific. As mentioned before, there is an exact relationship between the emotional quality of the experiences you have and the limiting beliefs that created them. Fearful thoughts produce fearful emotions, which produce a fear response in the field of intelligence, creating an event that will invoke the same kind of fear.

For example, if you have been living with an active vibration or thought habit of a fear of betrayal, you will make unconscious decisions and life will correspond through coincidences and synchronicities to materialize an event of betrayal. But even in the experiences you don't want, which are created by unintelligent thoughts or limiting beliefs, you are still experiencing a great blessing.

When you are aware that this is how the nature of reality works and that you are a powerful creator within the system, you can assume responsibility (an ability to respond) for the created experience. You can also use the event or circumstance or situation itself to deepen your self-awareness and use the tools you've learned to transform a fundamental aspect of yourself and the way you've been viewing the world, which hasn't served you. "What is it I've been thinking that has created this circumstance for me?" The problem becomes a gift when perceived by the enlightened person and is actually the way or the mechanism by which growth is achieved.

The Corresponding Nature of Life

Infinite Intelligence corresponds precisely to what you are thinking. This corresponding nature of life is the mechanism of coincidence and synchronicity. Whether you believe that money is hard to make, or health is your natural state, or people want to support you, or your voice and message is worthy to be heard—whether your beliefs are limiting or empowering—life will correspond to make the belief true for you. Sometimes life will confirm the thinking with a nearly instant manifestation. You think about someone and they call you. You need to hire a new resource and lo and behold someone applies even though the position isn't posted. You need a little bit of extra money and a rebate check comes in the mail.

The Echo Effect

At other times the mechanism of change can be slower, which can create a challenge and confusion for the person who has committed to a new decision. "I made a new decision; why do I keep getting more of the same?" What I have experienced in my own life and seen in the lives of my students is that there is a correlation between the amount of time it takes to change your circumstances or situation and the degree to which you've developed the habit of thought and emotion over the course of your life.

If the external changes in your reality are a reflection of the changes in your brain and your nervous system, then it would make sense that those beliefs that are long held, which are represented by neural networks that have more developed myelin and thicker, stronger synaptic connections, may need more time to fully evolve. While that neurophysiological evolution is happening, you may continue to get more of what you don't want, but only for a limited time.

The key here is to stay loyal to the decision and to the Higher Power System and not allow the circumstance that seems to represent the same ongoing pattern to deter you from the new momentum you're creating. It's important to understand now that this may occur in the future so you are properly prepared to hold firm as the change in your external reality progresses. In a sense what you may experience for a short period of time is what I call the Echo Effect—experiences created by your prior thinking that are just now realizing themselves even though you've made a new decision or have committed to the transformed belief.

In effect you are living in two distinct realities: the transformed reality of your new decision and the remnant reality of your prior limiting belief. Regardless of what shows up in your immediate reality, as long as you hold firm to the new decision while acknowledging that the current undesired experience is in the process of cycling out, you will be creating future experiences that align with the new decision. While doing so, it is possible to experience situations and circumstances that were already in the process of materialization. They are from previous thoughts and beliefs. The key is to know this as they are occurring. They should not be interpreted as evidence that your new decision somehow didn't stick with the universe or was in some way fallible or incorrect.

These Echo Effect experiences should simply be viewed as a remnant of your past limiting beliefs, cycling their way out, as the new decision becomes the predominant resonance of the circumstances of your future. The key is to relax through them. The mistake some people make when they experience the Echo Effect is to "undecide" and revert back to the limiting belief. *See, I knew it—you can't trust people. Life never works out for me. Good things happen but never last.* When the undesired experience occurs, just acknowledge that it is a part of your past, a memory, in the process of passing as your new decisions take hold.

The Bible speaks to this phenomenon when Jesus is on a ship with the disciples on the Sea of Galilee. A storm whips up and the disciples are afraid that it will wreck the boat. Jesus understands that a Higher Power is operating for him in intelligent and loving ways. In faith he climbs to the deck of the ship and rebukes (or denies) the winds, which immediately calm down. You, too, can deny the old patterns as they echo their way into your present experience, knowing that loyalty to your new decision will soon yield aligned, joyful, intelligent future experiences.

It is a good thing, actually, that there is a delay between the time we make a new decision and its realization. Imagine if manifestation were instantaneous. One negative thought could cause disaster for ourselves or others. You must think a thought habitually in order for it to have enough energy to take physical form. In a sense, the thought is a change request put into the system, and the system is using continued old experiences to confirm that you really want the change.

If you do the work and assert the new decision again even in the face of an experience that seems to represent your old limiting beliefs, you impress your will and your resonance on to the system to indicate, *Yes, I'm serious and committed to this change. This is what I truly believe.* From there, life has no alternative but to fulfill on the change request. Let the system work itself out while holding true to the new decision and, as law, the system must produce the desired change over time.

A Loving System

I briefly mentioned that the resonance or frequency of Infinite Intelligence or the Higher Power System is love and that it is always working for your greatest growth, your greatest prosperity, and your greatest evolution. What's more, it's operating in this form for all of us, all of humanity, simultaneously. It is using each individual in the system as an instrument to bring love, growth, and prosperity to all other members of the system—to the rest of humanity. I'll share a few examples.

Susan has been feeling like life isn't fair and that bad things happen to good people. Stephen has been feeling financially insecure and believes good things happen but don't last very long. Susan realizes that she's out of organic blueberries for her morning smoothie and decides to head to the grocery store to stock up. She plans on leaving at around 8:30 a.m. but gets a call from her sister that delays her departure by twenty minutes. That delay puts her on track for an unexpected rendezvous with Stephen, who has left his house to make the forty-five-minute drive to his new job. He's excited about it, it's been two weeks, and he desperately needed the job because he just moved into a larger, more expensive home to accommodate his girlfriend and her son.

Susan is at the grocery store and chooses a line that looks short but ends up taking a while because the woman in front of her decided to pay for her groceries with a check. Stephen ends up hitting just about every red light down the main strip toward his office and is now running ten minutes late. Susan's GPS gives her an alternative way to get home and she makes a right onto the same street that Stephen is traveling down and pulls out in front of Stephen. Nervous that this is the third time he's been late in two weeks, Stephen grabs his phone to text his manager that he's going to be a few minutes late, not realizing that traffic in front of him has come to a stop at a red light. As a result, he rear-ends Susan, and the incident and exchange of information takes an additional hour, causing Stephen to be late yet again, which results in his prompt termination.

Susan and Stephen, connected by the field of consciousness, co-created an experience that fulfilled on the more active beliefs that each of them had. Susan has been feeling like life isn't fair and that bad things happen to good people. Stephen has been feeling financially insecure and believes good things happen but don't last very long.

And it wasn't just Stephen and Susan who were involved in the play, but everyone and everything else that touched their experience. The woman who wrote the check, the line that Susan chose, her sister calling her at just the moment she had planned on leaving the house, the decision each driver was making that in aggregate created the entire traffic flow, the timing that was set for the stoplights—all these components were unconsciously decided by other people who played individual roles and contributed to the incident between Stephen and Susan. Not only that, but the timing of each of their decisions was the result of a nearly infinite number of moving pieces and decisions leading up to that present moment. In a way, all of history was coordinated to create that moment. Each person and each decision contributed to a moment in time that culminated in what seemed a tragic event for Susan and Stephen. But in this loving system there are no tragic events.

Both Susan and Stephen have also been desiring a change in their lives. Susan wants a life that is fair, which she can experience once she stops believing that life isn't fair. She wants good things to happen to good people, which they do, consistently, even though she doesn't see it that way. Stephen wants to be financially secure and this job he has isn't going to provide that for him, so life is trying to move him to a job (or perhaps even starting his own business) so that he can achieve financial security and freedom. Stephen wants good things to last forever and while change is inevitable, goodness can be a forever experience for him but only if he can change his beliefs. The car accident is the one moment of transformation that affords both Stephen and Susan the opportunity to realize that this experience is the same kind of experience that has been happening over and over for them their entire lives. If they were in this work they might ask, "How did I create this?" They could then use the experience to notice their beliefs and leverage the tools we teach to transform them, thus changing their future and changing themselves.

That is what life is encouraging us all to do when we're faced with the challenging and undesired experiences of our lives.

Every experience we have is an act of love encouraging us toward the change we deeply desire. I've had students and friends tell me that cancer, addiction, bankruptcy, divorce, or losing their jobs or homes was the best thing that happened to them. If the circumstances of your life always went the way you wanted them to, you would never grow. It is only through the challenges that you are able to increase your capacity, and it is only through an increased capacity that you are able to achieve the great vision you have for your life. You become stronger, kinder, calmer, more courageous, empathetic, compassionate, and powerful by transforming and translating the uncomfortable experiences of your life. The difficult experiences you have aren't roadblocks to the life you desire; they are the road itself.

Tragedy

Even in what seem to be the greatest tragedies we find that life is working for our greatest growth, our greatest prosperity, and our greatest evolution. The superorganism of consciousness is constantly expanding and, by extension, encouraging us into becoming more evolved, loving, and connected human beings. Just as the promises of recovery become available to the struggling addict when they hit bottom, so too does the promise of an evolved consciousness realize itself through the challenges, tragedies, and perceived problems of the world.

When I was living in Orlando, Florida, in 2016, a gunman opened fire on club-goers at Pulse nightclub in an act of homophobia, killing forty-nine and wounding fifty-three others. It was a horrible, senseless tragedy. Soon after my wife and I were walking around the lake at the center of the downtown area. "How could life always be working for us, when we witness such a violent tragedy?" she asked. "Surely this can't be the act of a loving, intelligent system."

As we continued our walk, discussing the merits of the methodology in relation to the experienced atrocities of the world, we overheard other people talking about the incident. As we listened, we heard people say things like, "Wow, I never knew there was so much hatred toward the gay community," or, "Something has to be done; nobody should feel unsafe because of their identity." Consciousness was awakening on a mass scale as a result of the Pulse nightclub shooting, and in that elevated awareness change began to take place. New legislation was passed protecting the LGBTQ+ community. The greater Orlando community came together in an incredible display of love and acceptance for a group that had been the victim of prejudice for decades. Ten thousand people gathered in a march showing solidarity and unity for the LGBTQ+ community as a result of the terrible calamity of that one night.

Were it not for our misunderstanding and fear of the unknown around death, and for the true emotional loss that is felt when a loved one leaves the physical body, we would have a much easier time understanding how All That Is works as our greatest teacher. We avoid future Holocausts because of the great suffering of the Nazi genocide against the Jews. We stand for the liberation and protection of children everywhere as a result of our becoming aware of the inexplicable horrors of the global child-trafficking industry. We celebrate and protect the power and rights of all women as a result of becoming aware of the abusive working conditions and sexual harassment they've been forced to endure. We create better global systems as a result of becoming aware of how predatory and corrupt the current financial, pharmaceutical, media, military, and governance systems function. This is the process of civilization.

There are no problems.
Nothing ever goes wrong.

We see the possibility of an expanded humanity and world as a result of experiencing the dynamic of a contrasted and contracted one. In each individual experience we perceive as a tragedy (losing a loved one, a marriage, or a fortune) and in each collective experience we perceive as a tribulation (a recession, a pandemic, or an act of terror) we find the infinitely intelligent seeds of love being planted to direct us toward a higher frequency. Toward greater joy and ultimately better lives— whether in this life or the next. Our attachment to this life rather than our understanding that, as consciousness, we entertain many lives is what creates the perception of "bad things" or "problems."

When we remove the attachment to this life and accept the idea that we are each coming into this life to experience our part of an expanded consciousness through the dynamic experiences of our lives, very much like a video game with an infinite number of lives, we can ease ourselves into the idea that the system, in its entirety, is loving. There are no problems, and nothing ever goes wrong. Life is constantly working us toward even greater expansion and understanding, even and especially in death, pain, suffering, and sorrow. The wound really is the way.

Death and Grieving

For fourteen years a small five-and-a-half-pound Chihuahua named Dexter graced my side. Everywhere I went, like a shadow, I was followed by my furry friend. I often carried Dexter in my left arm, which is where he also sat anytime we'd go for a drive, giving him the perfect view out the driver-side window. When I lost Dexter to old age, heart disease, and kidney failure, it was devastating. The absence of Dexter from my arms was traumatic, as he had spent so much time there over the decade and a half prior. I felt like I had lost a limb. The feeling was emotional, it was physical, it was incredibly painful, and it was real.

After two days of nonstop suffering, in a small gap that opened up outside my missing Dexter, I had a thought: *I wonder what the methodology would say about this.* Clearly I was in suffering, and by any reasonable person's observation it was a well-justified misery. But I was in a Primal state, and I wondered if all the pain I was experiencing wasn't from the absence of Dexter but rather the presence of unintelligent thinking, and whether the framework would not only hold true but support me in accessing an even deeper level of self-awareness around what was really causing my pain, and potentially, a revelation or breakthrough.

I decided to use the tools that I teach and began by realizing that I was in a Primal state. There was no doubt about the level of suffering I was experiencing and the misery that had engulfed me for the prior few days. I knew that my suffering was separate from the experience. As dramatic and shocking as death is, loss of a loved one is not an exception to universal laws and as such I knew that the suffering I was experiencing was separate from the physical loss of my beloved dog.

I also knew that the cause of my suffering was one thing, and one thing only: the beliefs, thoughts, or meaning I was giving to the experience. I took a moment to observe my mind, to see what I was thinking and, in particular, which thoughts were causing me the most suffering. I grabbed my journal and divided the page into three columns—the first for my limiting beliefs, the second for my new decision, and the third for the evidence to support my new decision. I slowly penned the first limiting belief that came to mind.

Dexter should have lived longer.

I contemplated this for a brief moment, looking at it through the lens of knowing that if this thought caused me suffering it wasn't true. And of course, it wasn't. I wrote my new decision, and what was really true, in the second column.

Dexter died precisely when he should have.

He had a long life (which is in fact irrelevant but I allowed it to be somewhat comforting) and as he began to experience heart disease and kidney failure it was time to put him down. In the third column, I wrote down what evidence I had for the fact that Dexter died precisely when he should have.

Because he died, I wrote.

Sometimes the evidence is self-evident. How do I know he died when he was supposed to? Because that's when he died. Even in my misery, I was able to acknowledge that when someone's time comes, it comes, and the timing of it isn't up to me. But just the thought that Dexter should have somehow lived longer than he did made me feel cheated. It caused me to feel like life was unfair. Just taking a moment to see the unintelligence of my thinking freed me from a portion of the suffering I was experiencing.

I searched for the next thought that was causing me pain and realized that *this* thought was the true cause of the deepest level of pain I was experiencing.

I'm never going to see Dexter again.

I wrote the belief down in the first column. Even at the level of familiarity I had with the methodology, I wasn't sure what to do next. There didn't seem to be anything unintelligent about this idea. Dexter was gone, and I had no evidence to believe there was any possibility of seeing him again. But suffering can do something extraordinary to an individual, especially if you have a trusted tool that time and time again has helped you see the truth. It compels you to be open, and open I was. But I needed some coaching.

Okay, David, listen, you know how this works, I said to myself. *If the belief that I'm never going to see Dexter again is causing me to move into a Primal state, then it's not true and some form of the opposite must be true.*

I thought for a moment before hesitantly writing down my new empowered decision.

I am going to see Dexter again.

I sat staring at the third column, unsure of what to do next. I waited for the evidence to show up, but nothing in my personal experience supported the idea that, after someone's dog dies, they will see them again. I sat in the space of inquiry for a bit. *What evidence do I have that this is true?* I repeated the question over and over again. I knew that if I just stayed in the frequency of the question, an idea, a thought, or an answer would come. But nothing had come…yet.

A few days later I was going for a walk and an idea seemingly came out of nowhere. There are people who have had what's called a "near death experience." Sometimes for five, ten, even twenty minutes people have been declared clinically dead but somehow return to life. I remembered seeing some YouTube videos where these people shared what their story was like and the details of their crossing over to the other side. I pulled my phone out of my pocket, did a quick search for "near death experience dogs," and started scanning the search results.

I found a woman in her mid-fifties with a blog where she had written a post about how she drowned, died for seven minutes, and what she experienced on the other side. In her story she shared that she was greeted by her collie who had passed a few years earlier. She shared her story about how amazing it was to see her beloved friend again. She went on to describe many other incredible details about what happens in the afterlife, but what struck me was how consciousness had guided me to this blog post simply through my willingness to work the Decision Matrix and to sit in an inquiry around "what evidence do I have that this is true." That question inspired access to the idea of near-death experiences, which then led me to the blog post evidencing that it's possible that I *would* see Dexter again, in the life after.

The power of this methodology isn't just the transformed belief. It's the possibility of experiencing a massive revelation and expansion in the way you think as a result of the *elimination* of the limiting belief. Yes, I had just realized that the physical absence of Dexter wasn't the cause of my discomfort; it was thinking that I'd never see him again. And in the process of using the methodology I created the possibility, for myself, that I might see Dexter again in some form of afterlife, just like the woman who had died and come back. But it was what happened after freeing myself from my suffering that was the true breakthrough. Once I was no longer entangled with my limiting belief, I was able to ask some powerful questions and, as a result, gain some life-changing insights.

If the system is loving, I thought, *and if nothing ever goes wrong and there are no problems, why* does *the system include death rather than no death?* In other words, if the system is perfect, wouldn't it have been better to create a reality where dogs lived forever? Or for that matter that I could live forever with Dexter? Why wait until the afterlife to reunite me with my friend? There had to be a reason for death that was more love-based and complex than simply a biological explanation. If there are no mistakes in the divine perfection of how the system functions, why death?

After a few minutes of contemplation, it hit me. I was overwhelmed with the realization and the flood of gratitude that engulfed me. In my exploration around my suffering related to Dexter's death, I experienced a radical revelation not just about Dexter but about the reason why the universe, God, consciousness, or Higher Power created the mechanism of life and death in the first place.

I loved my Dexter. My love for my dog was unconditional. And in my own mind there was no way I could have possibly loved him more than I already did. *Until* I experienced the absence of him. Having experienced Dexter in the physical and *then* experiencing the absence of Dexter in the physical exponentially expanded my love for my dog. I thought I loved my dog, but it was nothing compared to the love I felt in his absence. That's when it hit me.

What an incredibly perfect and loving system we live in. The system is perfect. And even in death it is working for us. Because now, as a result of my expanded love for my dog, which could only occur in his absence, I believe that after I leave the physical I'll spend the rest of eternity with Dexter with a love that I could never have experienced had he lived for-ever—an eternity of expanded love with your best friend. Not only with Dexter, but with *everyone* I've ever loved. That, friend, is a perfect, loving, and intelligent system.

17

The Power of a Changed Mind

For a long while, I thought I needed a "perfect" mindset. I had this idea that as long as I had any limiting beliefs it would be difficult if not impossible to create what I wanted in the areas of my life where I was engaged in unintelligent thinking. Beliefs are so powerful that if you believe you have to have a perfect mindset to create change, well then that's true for you. The good news is that it's not *inherently* true. You don't need a perfect mindset. News flash: nobody has one.

The primal parts of your nervous system are always going to be on high alert for threats, and that's a good thing. Just in case you end up in an actual life-threatening situation, you'll have the system you need to react effectively to live another day. Your unintelligent thinking and fears and worries are always going to be a part of you; they just don't have to drive the bus. By making just small changes to your mindset, you can effect radical transformation in your external reality.

The resonance of an intelligent thought is far more powerful than an unintelligent one.

A little bit of improved money consciousness goes a long way. Being just a tad more open to things not needing to be hard can create tremendous ease in your life. Relaxing just a little bit around your health, relationship, or business problem by doing the work and using the tools in this book can produce massive shifts in every area of your life.

The resonance of an intelligent thought is far more powerful than an unintelligent one. You need only make small, on-the-margin changes in the way you think to begin to see dramatic shifts. And once you begin to experience the changes in your life due to the small pivots in your mind, it gets even easier and easier to make more and more mental shifts. This is the reason why in Matthew 17:20 (NIV) it is written, *Truly I tell you, if you have faith as small as a mustard seed, you can say to this mountain, "Move from here to there," and it will move. Nothing will be impossible for you.* The system does not require perfection of you. It simply requires small shifts in the way you think, feel, and perceive reality, and reality will confirm in broad, sweeping, and astounding ways to those inner adjustments. It simply requires the faith of a mustard seed.

A Framework for Daily Living

Ultimately you are responsible. And that's a great thing. It's the source of all your power. You have an ability to respond to any thought, feeling, circumstance, or situation in your life. After all, you created it, so you have the power to change it. As you apply the tools and technologies of *A Changed Mind*, you'll find rapid, profound shifts occurring almost instantaneously. Will your entire life change immediately? No, of course not. Change does take time. It's neurophysiological.

It took you decades to build the neuropathways that are driving your thoughts, emotions, and vibration. But it doesn't take decades to rewire them. No matter how long you've been experiencing bad relationships, no matter how long you've been feeling anxious or depressed, regardless of what the doctors or experts said, and notwithstanding how bad your childhood trauma or abuse was, small changes can happen in an instant. Profound, sweeping changes can happen over a relatively short period of time, especially when you make this work a primary focus in your life. And particularly if you choose to make your relationship with yourself, others, and the system itself a daily, living practice.

There is no practice more important than taking note of how you feel on a moment-by-moment basis and, when you've moved into a Primal state, doing the work to move back into a Powerful state of being. The goal should not be to live consistently in a Powerful state. There are always going to be moments or experiences that trigger your limiting beliefs, or fears, or some uncomfortable memory from the past. But with consistent application of the methodology you'll quickly find yourself moving into a Primal state less frequently and spending less time in suffering when it does occur.

There is a direct correlation between the amount of time you spend in a Powerful state and the level of joy, wealth, health, connection, energy, and resourcefulness you experience in your life. The road to your full potential and the life you've always dreamed of is paved with Powerful states. And you now have the understanding and the tools to grow in your capacity to consistently align yourself with the power of Intelligence itself.

While a changed mind doesn't happen overnight, each time you apply the tools you eliminate old neural networks that represent the limiting beliefs that don't serve you and build new networks for your new empowered decisions. Having a daily practice or ritual (I'll share mine with you in a moment) can help you accelerate the process. However, unlike meditation, breathwork, chanting, journaling, or other great transformational tools that have their dedicated time and uses, this methodology is meant to be taken on the road with you and into the daily experiences and challenges of your life. The work is best done in the real-time moments of your daily living. That's the beauty of this practice. You do the reps in the midst of your life, not apart from it. Each time you notice that you've moved into a Primal state, you're making progress. Each time you identify the unintelligent thinking that's creating your suffering, you're doing the work. Every opportunity you have to question your thinking and make a new decision, you're making huge strides forward. Every time you find evidence for the fact that your new decision is true, you're changing your brain and yourself. The key to rapid growth and closing the gap between where you are and who you are, and where and who you want to be, is to make this work your living spiritual practice. Every day. One day at a time.

My wife is exceptionally well organized. Thanks to her, everything in our home has its place. Early on in our relationship, I would come home from a long day's work, kick off my shoes near the front door, walk over to the sofa, plunge myself into the relaxing cushions, and kick my feet up on the coffee table. And when I say "kick off my shoes," I mean *kick off my shoes*. One shoe might be upturned sideways in the middle of the foyer. The other may have made it near the shoe rack at the entrance, maybe not (more likely thrown on top of all the pairs of my wife's nicely aligned shoes). But no big deal. I had worked a long day and deserved to kick up my heels and relax a little bit. Or so I thought.

For months this habit of mine of coming home and tossing my shoes in the entryway became a sticking point for Carol and me. I felt entitled to do whatever I wanted to do with my shoes. After all, they weren't hurting anyone. There weren't any guests coming over to the house. What was the big deal? For Carol, it *was* a big deal. And she left no room for any doubt about the fact that it was not acceptable. We battled over the shoes for months until one day on my way home from work, in anticipation of the conflict, I had a revelation as a result of working the Mind Hack Method.

On my way home I played through the scenario in my head, which was not difficult given how many times it had actually happened. Clearly in the moment of conflict I was in a Primal state. So I took a moment to reflect on the thoughts that I had in the moment of conflict. When I looked at the thinking I discovered that I believed *Carol shouldn't be angry with me*. What was revelatory for me was that Carol actually being angry with me wasn't causing my suffering; it was *believing* she "shouldn't be angry with me" when she was. I worked a mental Decision Matrix and came up with a simple, straightforward new decision. I wasn't quite sure where it was going, but the process was simple. I made a mental note of my new decision: *Carol should be angry with me*.

I didn't have total clarity of where this was going but stuck to the process. Only one step left: What evidence did I have that this was true, that Carol should be angry with me for leaving my shoes in the middle of the entryway? Well, that was simple. Because someone as organized as Carol, who has her own emotionally triggering memories and beliefs around disorder and chaos, would absolutely get angry about me throwing my shoes into the middle of the room.

She's an amazing wife, keeps a tidy home, and spends a lot of time and energy to create a feeling of organization so that our home is peaceful, beautiful, and we can find the things we need easily because they're always put back in the same place. In seeing how much Carol cared about the home, and me, I realized that I had been uncaring and self-centered. I didn't want to upset my wife. She was far more important to me than not taking an extra few seconds to put my shoes on the shoe rack. Of course she should be upset with me given who she is, how she thinks, and what's important to her.

I came home that night, opened the door quietly, slipped off my shoes, and placed them perfectly on the rack. Carol was on the computer paying some bills. I put my hands on her shoulders, kissed her on the back of the head, and apologized.

"I'm sorry about not appreciating how well you take care of our home, and me," I said. "I've been a real jerk about that shoe thing, and I want to let you know that I want to make things as easy as I can for you. You do a lot to keep the home organized, and I'm going to do my best to support you in that. I'm sorry."

I'm not sure Carol knew how to respond, because it was such a break of our usual pattern. (You, too, may find in circumstances like this that your partner may not initially react with flowers and fanfare.) But how someone else reacts isn't actually important. What's important is your capacity to use the methodology to see your own unintelligent thinking and, in the moment of breakthrough and seeing what you've been doing, elevate yourself to a much higher quality of character, emotional experience, and presence for others.

Each time we choose to use the tools and apply them to the experiences of our life, we grow. It's like going to the gym and doing one more repetition. Over time we build stronger and stronger emotional muscle, greater and greater compassion and empathy, and peel back the layers of limiting belief, stories, and unintelligence that are preventing us from being the best we can be for ourselves and the people we love most. One rep at a time.

The Mind Hack Method Living Practice

Step 1: Notice that you've moved into a Primal state or some form of suffering, stress, anxiety, overwhelm, and so forth.

Step 2: Identify the specific thinking or belief that is causing you suffering and acknowledge that it must not be true (it is unintelligent) because it doesn't feel good.

Step 3: If the limiting belief isn't true, some form of the opposite must be true. Make a new decision that is aligned with the outcome you want and that feels good.

Step 4: Find evidence for the fact that your new decision is true.

The Mind Hack Morning Ritual

When most people first get into this work, there's a backlog of limiting beliefs to identify and transform. Like a garden that's been untended for years, our minds have accumulated significant bramble and weed, and most of our students want to find a way to make some initial headway to clear the brush. In addition to applying the methodology as a daily living practice to the present moment of your life, you can also dedicate twenty to thirty minutes each morning to rewire your brain using the tools you've learned from this book.

The Mind Hack Morning Ritual is designed to help you identify any resistance you may have and to clear it out so you aren't carrying it into your day. It's also structured to prime the electrical circuits of your brain and nervous system with emotional states and images that are conducive to the kind of day and future you want to create. When you remove resistance by pruning the neural networks that represent your limiting beliefs and spend dedicated time each day building new neural pathways to reflect the new thoughts, emotions, and real-world experiences and results you want to create, you can radically accelerate a changed mind.

If you're wanting to become more self-aware, identify and eliminate your limiting beliefs, reduce the amount of time you spend in stress, anxiety, or overwhelm, dramatically improve your emotional and spiritual experience of life, and begin to create massive shifts in your external reality, the Mind Hack Morning Ritual is a must-have practice to start your day.

Step 1: Morning Decision Matrix

Like many people, you may wake up in the morning already feeling stressed, which can lead to a feeling of defeat from the very get-go. First, let me say that there's nothing wrong with you. Most people have been experiencing stress for so long that the body can become habituated to it. Without any external trigger, you can simply become so used to the stress that you wake up in a Primal state. Conversely, you may be someone who wakes up feeling energized and grateful but as the day wanes it also wears on you, and by the time you get halfway through the day or certainly by the end of your day your morning gratitude and Powerful state may have faded into a smoldering state of suffering.

Either way, waking up with a process to clean the slate (or baseline your vibration) can be a day saver. For the first twelve months after my recovery I used the Mind Hack Morning Ritual every single day to get my mind right from the start. The first step is to grab your journal and to notice if you're feeling any tension, sadness, stress, anxiety, or any primal emotions. If you aren't, that's great and you can move right on to the second part of the Mind Hack Morning Ritual. If you are, take five minutes to write down what you're thinking and feeling. Unlike a standard Decision Matrix, you don't have to identify any limiting beliefs yet. Simply write out everything you're thinking in your journal, almost like a rant, until you feel a little bit of relief now that you've gotten it down on paper. Just the process of taking the fast-moving thoughts and slowing them down and getting them in front of you on paper can be transformative and relieving.

Once you've got your thoughts in front of you, identify three to five of the statements or limiting beliefs that feel strongest to you (in other words, that feel like they're causing the most suffering) and *then* work a Decision Matrix on those three to five thoughts. That's Step 1: journal out your stress, cherry-pick a few of the big limiting beliefs, and work a Decision Matrix. The total time to do both parts should require only about ten to fifteen minutes. By the time you're done you'll feel a significant shift in the way you're feeling.

As you work the Decision Matrix, you'll move out of a Primal state and into a Powerful state, which is the foundation of emotion we want for the next step of the ritual. In the beginning it can feel like there's a lot to work through or that the same limiting beliefs are coming up each day. Don't worry, that's normal. Take it one day at a time and do a little bit of work each day and within thirty days you'll notice a massive clearing of decades of limiting belief buildup.

Step 2: Gratitude Journaling

Now that you're in a Powerful state and you've cleared out some of the morning cobwebs, take another five minutes to list out ten to twenty things you're grateful for. You want to supercharge your nervous system, which you can do more easily now that you've offloaded so much resistance. Don't worry about whether you *feel* grateful enough or not. This isn't a contest. The point is to just get your mind focused on paying attention to what you like, and the best way to do that is to bring to mind those things that you're grateful for.

As you learned in the Mind Hack Method, gratitude is one of the most effective ways for increasing your energy. Each day, the challenges, people, circumstances, and situations ahead of you will become opportunities and gifts if you can bring enough energy to them. Morning gratitude infused into your nervous system will create right perception for the day. Perhaps it's a good night's sleep, your home, your furry friend, your job, someone you love, appreciation for yourself, for working on yourself, the smell of your morning coffee, whatever. Ride the Powerful state that you created as a result of doing your Morning Decision Matrix and elevate your energy through a short gratitude rampage. If you write down the same thing you wrote down the day before, that's fine too. You can never be too grateful for the things you love in your life, including yourself!

Step 3: Visualization

Now that you've taken some time to remove the layer of resistance and have brought your focus and energy toward those things you appreciate and want more of, you've set the stage for building new future memories through the power of imagination and visualization. Remember that your brain doesn't know the difference between imagination and reality, and investing a little bit of dedicated time each morning to build and reinforce the images you have of your future is a powerful mind hack and catalyst for accelerating the realization of those future events and experiences.

When I first came to understand the power of visualization I struggled, thinking that I wasn't a particularly good "visualizer." What I've learned over time is that everyone starts out their visualization experience a little bit differently. Some people are very visual and can see the images in their mind's eye. Other people seem to "talk" through the future scenes in their head and describe what it might look like rather than see what it looks like. Some people are very connected to the emotion of the experience while others are more cognitive or heady. What's important to understand is that there isn't a better or worse way to visualize, and you can't get it wrong. The only mistake you can make is to not commit to your visualization practice because you think you're not doing it well or doing it right.

If you're willing to simply spend five minutes imagining, as best as you can, the experiences you want in your future, over time you'll develop an even greater capacity to tap into all forms and ways of visualizing. When my wife and I first started visualizing together, she would come out of her visualizations like she was on some sort of magical four-dimensional carpet ride. I on the other hand didn't really see or feel much. But just like any new activity, over time I started developing more capacity to get into deeper visualizations, and it wasn't long before I was having full-color mind-blowing experiences of my future life and self.

The goal of the Mind Hack Morning Ritual is to be simple enough and quick enough that you can do it every day. All you need is a five-minute visualization to get your nervous system and brain primed with your potential future. You can do the same visualization every day or you can switch it up. I prefer to listen to inspirational instrumental music to accompany my visualizations, usually movie themes or classical pieces, but you can use whatever music genre you prefer or no music at all.

Set your clock for five minutes and enjoy whatever unfolds. Begin to think about things you desire in the future. Perhaps you imagine yourself at a book signing, speaking from stage, relaxing with your loved one, giving birth to your first child, attending their first sporting event, having your company ringing the opening bell at the stock market. You can have multiple vignettes in your visualization or just go deep on one scene. None of that matters. What matters is that you get into the habit of using your brain the way it's meant to be used—in this case to consciously create new neural networks that represent the future you desire. As you visualize, you'll continue to elevate your energy as you move into the final step of the Mind Hack Morning Ritual and prepare yourself for a powerful day.

Step 4: Mindfulness Meditation

The last step of the Mind Hack Morning Ritual is designed to slow down the normal mental chatter and to further develop your capacity to be observant and aware of your thoughts. There are many forms of meditation or mindfulness, and if you have a specific practice by all means continue with that practice. What we are wanting to do is bring calm to the nervous system, and that is achieved through breathing, stillness, and not allowing our thoughts to create emotional triggers or responses. Achieving this is quite simple.

Find a quiet place where you can sit in a chair (or cross-legged if that's comfortable for you). The key is to be in a physically comfortable position and to have your spine upright. Set your timer for five minutes and over time work your way up to a twenty-minute meditation. Again you can use music if you'd like, but I'd recommend something soothing, quiet, and instrumental or no music at all. You don't want your mind to attach to the music or any memories associated with it. It should be used to simply contribute to the relaxed mood and environment.

Start by resting your hands in your lap faced upward or comfortably crossed and take a few deep inhales and exhales to relax your body. Notice your feet supported by the floor beneath you, and scan your body to see if there's any tension.

Just notice and continue to relax the body as you bring your focus and attention on your breath. Don't try to alter your breathing; just notice it. The body breathes at its own cadence. All you're wanting to do is pay attention to it. You may notice it change as you bring your attention to it, or it may stay the same. There's literally nothing to do here other than to observe your body doing what it does every day all day—breathe. The objective here is to simply calm down the thought process and relax the body so you can train your nervous system and your mind away from reactivity and toward stillness. This will allow you to create space in your day-to-day experiences for responding to life in new ways rather than reacting to it out of your old habits.

You've done an incredible job clearing out the limiting beliefs that had shown up that morning using the Decision Matrix in Step 1. That process released a ton of energy that you directed into gratitude and appreciation to further the development of your brain toward the kinds of emotions, ideas, and things you desire. From there you rode that wave of Powerful states into a visualization process to continue to grow and evolve your brain and you in the direction of your desired future. And now with a final mindfulness meditation you are bringing it all to a close with a relaxation and stillness process that will give you a greater sense of awareness and connection with yourself and with spirit as you move into your day.

This twenty to thirty-minute morning routine has changed the lives of myself and thousands of our students. The first few times may feel like a little bit of effort. You may experience some initial resistance because, like anything new, you're activating parts of your body and neurology that have been habituated to very active sympathetic patterns for many, many years. But if you can commit to just seven days, then perhaps thirty, your entire morning, day, and attitude will radically shift and the results will begin to manifest themselves in profound ways into the moments and experiences of your daily life.

If you're really serious about change, the best thing you can do is surround yourself with other people who are headed in the same direction as you are. This book is a tool not only for you but for the people around you who are also seeking the next level of transformation. My recommendation: give this book as a gift of transformation and get yourself a Mind Hack Morning Ritual partner. Commit to doing the ritual for thirty days together, and check in daily or every other day as you progress. Sharing the discoveries, breakthroughs, and changes you experience in your inner and outer world is the best way to reinforce that change. From addiction recovery to personal growth to becoming a Phenomenon, every step of my journey has been accelerated because I did it in fellowship with others. You have someone, or a few people, in your life right now who are asking for a change in their lives. Let you and this book be the answer to their asking and surround yourself with friends, family, employees, and partners who are committed to a changed mind.

Do your Mind Hack Morning Ritual on the days that you don't feel you have the time to do it. As Gandhi once famously said, *I have so much to accomplish today that I must meditate for two hours instead of one.* Gandhi knew that his ability to create space, calm, and joy and get his mind right was the key to succeeding in his most busy and challenging days. You don't have to live in an ashram in order to find psychological peace. You can simply spend twenty minutes in the morning engaged in your Mind Hack Morning Ritual and bring your inner yogi with you so that regardless of what shows up, you stay unshaken amidst the dynamic experiences of the world.

As I mentioned, a great way to do this practice is to find an accountability partner and work a seven, ten, or thirty-day Mind Hack challenge. Finding a partner is easy. You can gift this book to a friend and do the daily ritual together. Or, if you have purchased our full Mind Hack Program (www.DavidBayer.com/MindHack), you can find an accountability partner in the private members area.

18

Your Time Is Now

The world seems like it's moving faster and becoming more chaotic by the day. It can feel like we have less control over our own lives, our finances, our health, and our families and that external forces have a greater influence on us than ever before. But that's only true if that's what you believe. What I believe is that humanity is undergoing a radical transformation. In every breakdown, even a global one, the space is created for a new emergence.

Consciousness is evolving. The human species is evolving. Having the tools to stay on the leading edge of that evolution is what will carry us forward. The ability to manage your mind, to control your nervous system, and to be psychologically and emotionally fit amidst the change is more important now than ever before. Not just so you can navigate the challenges but so you can lead your family, your friends, your employees, your spiritual community, and all the people you interact with and influence into the new world and new consciousness that is arising out of our current one. That is arising through *you*.

You are a powerful creator, and as you learn how to reengineer the chaos of your own life, you transform the chaos in the world. As we, together, as a community and tribe, commit ourselves to the spiritual practice of taking radical responsibility for the experiences of our lives and use the teachings and tools in this book to change the way we think, feel, and act, together, *we* change the world.

All the problems in the world have been created by people operating from a Primal state and engaging in unintelligent thinking. Happy people don't do bad things, and as you learn how to operate from joy, compassion, curiosity—from a Powerful state—regardless of the circumstance or situation, you not only change your reality but you transform the collective consciousness and your co-created reality. You become the change you want to see in the world. As you awaken to the truth that Intelligence is always working for your greatest growth, your greatest prosperity, and your greatest evolution, and as you learn to live life from that perspective, you become an agent of change and a force for good not only for yourself but for all humanity.

You are now ready, more than ever, to be a force for good. You have the knowledge, the tools, and the desire to have a powerful living experience. You have the ability to share your transformation through the evidence of your own life and the simple tool of this book. You are the answer to someone else's prayer or question to the universe: *How can I create more powerfully in my life and end my personal suffering?* And as your consciousness continues to evolve, you become an example to the next person of what's really possible. You become an example of what it means to rise to a new level of human.

I've been so blessed by this work. It's changed my life forever. There was a time when I lived in constant suffering, and while I'm by no means perfect at living in a Powerful state, I can tell you that I do the best I can each and every day to continue to work on myself, and as a result I've created a life with more joy, more connection, more love, and more abundance than I could have ever imagined.

And if I can do it, then you can do it. And if we can do it, then we *all* can do it. The change that you and I want to see in the world, it starts with us. It spreads one person at a time. This book and these teachings are the flame that we can pass from one person to the next. As much as I've shared my story with you, this book certainly isn't about me. Truth be told, even though my intention was to write for you in each and every writing session, this book really isn't about you either. It's about a movement.

There is a beautiful splintering in the world right now. The old world is represented by a humanity that lives in a Primal state. The new humanity are people like you and me and so many others who are coming together to be a part of the solution, starting with ourselves. To transcend and transform the pain and suffering in our own lives so that we can represent the possibility of living in a Powerful state and to help those who still suffer find their way to the promise of a changed mind.

I want to invite you to be a part of this movement. You've made it this far, after all. I invite you to join myself, my family, my team, and my tribe in ending all human suffering. To be a part of a community and a family that supports each other, together, as we elevate ourselves and change the world. Not through addressing the challenges and the contrast of the world, but by creating something new from a Powerful state of being. At the center of this movement is an understanding of who you are and how we are going to evolve, to the next level, together.

The Next Step

Staying connected to this community is the key to sustained transformation. And going deeper into this work will help to connect you to others who are committed to growth as well as accelerate your own. Below are a list of key resources that I invite you to take advantage of, many of which are free.

Free Trainings and Weekly Motivation, Personal Growth, and Inspiration

For starters, visit my website www.DavidBayer.com. There you'll find a variety of free trainings on everything from mindset to business, wealth, relationships, and health. Subscribe to our email list. You'll get weekly content as this work continues to evolve and access to bonus trainings, special events, and opportunities to connect and go deeper. You'll also get access to any free online communities we've started on Facebook or other platforms.

Business and Mindset Coaching Programs

If you really want to develop personal mastery, there's no better way than to work with a mentor or coach. Whether you want to go deeper on getting support for your mindset and achieving your personal goals or you're interested in our mindset and business coaching programs for entrepreneurs, we would love to explore how my team of coaches can support you in changing your mind and achieving your next-level goals. To learn more about our coaching programs, visit www.DavidBayer. com/Coaching.

Coaching and Leadership Certification Programs

If you're interested in becoming certified in our methodologies, whether you're a coach, consultant, leader, or simply want to make a greater impact on the lives of those around you, we offer a certification program several times a year. Visit www.DavidBayer.com/Certifications to learn more.

Live Events and Seminars

Come join us for three life-changing days at our annual event, The Powerful Living Experience Live. The event was named "a top 3 must attend personal development event" by *Inc.* magazine. You can see dates, details, and check out live footage from the event at www. PowerfulLivingExperience.com.

Social Media and Podcast

For daily inspiration and to be even more connected to our community, find me on Instagram, Facebook, and YouTube in addition to subscribing to my podcast, which you can find on Apple or Spotify, or visit www. DavidBayer.com for links to all my social channels.

Share Your Experiences

Let your transformation be a light and motivation for others. Share your breakthroughs on social media, gift this book to a friend, recommend it online, post a review on Amazon, and email us at support@davidbayer.com with your experience of reading this book and the results it has brought into your mind and your life.

And Lastly...

Congratulations. I want to acknowledge you and thank you for doing what many have had the opportunity to do but few have actually done. You've taken a step across the threshold into a new life, new relationships, and new possibilities. You've done the work, invested the time and energy, and been open to new ideas and new knowledge. Is this the end of the journey? Of course not—it's just the beginning. But as a result of the simple act of getting to this point, you've already become a different person. Haven't you?

Change is inevitable once you become willing to change. You're on your way to becoming happier, wealthier, healthier, and fully alive. Not because you learned how to solve all your problems, figured out how to make it all happen, or discovered how to change your circumstances. You're on your way because you understand that you are responsible. That you are capable. That you truly are powerful.

Will it feel like that every day? Certainly not. But each time you apply one of the distinctions in this book, you're taking one more step toward a new you. Each time you see your unintelligent thinking as unintelligent, or you express gratitude in the face of problems, or you make a new decision contrary to your old limiting belief, you are changing.

I think that sometimes we make the mistake of thinking that change happens in some big, sweeping, full-of-fanfare type of miraculous experience. Sometimes it does. But mostly it doesn't. It happens over the course of the small shifts in the daily decisions, thoughts, and feelings that we choose to have.

Yes—you get to choose. Nobody can do it for you. AND…you can do it. I know you can. If I can do it, you can do it. Trust me! Everything you want is right in front of you right now. It's just one thought away. I can't wait to see what you decide to do next. It all starts with a changed mind.